Corporate
Real Estate
Handbook

Corporate Real Estate Handbook

Robert A. Silverman

Editor-in-Chief

McGraw-Hill Book Company
New York   St. Louis   San Francisco   Auckland
Bogotá   Hamburg   Johannesburg   London   Madrid
Mexico   Milan   Montreal   New Delhi   Panama
Paris   São Paulo   Singapore
Sydney   Tokyo   Toronto

Library of Congress Cataloging-in-Publication Data

Corporate real estate handbook.

Includes index.
1. Commercial buildings.   2. Industrial buildings.
3. Office buildings.   4. Real estate business.
I. Silverman, Robert A., 1947–
HD1393.25.C67   1987   658.2   86-15337
ISBN 0-07-045900-2

ISBN 0-07-045900-2

*The editors for this book were Martha Jewett and Jim Bessent,
the designer was Naomi Auerbach, and the production
supervisor was Teresa F. Leaden. It was set in
Baskerville by University Graphics, Inc.*

Printed and bound by R. R. Donnelley & Sons Company.

Contents

About the Editor

Robert A. Silverman is director of planning for Harvard University. He was formerly vice president of Harvard's real estate subsidiary and has also served as a financial analyst at the university. He earned his Ph.D. degree there as well. In addition, Mr. Silverman is a director of NACORE, the International Association of Corporate Real Estate Executives.

Contributors

H. Dennis Boyle is a vice president in the financial services group of Cushman & Wakefield, Inc. He is a member of the American Institute of Real Estate Appraisers (MAI), Chairman of NACORE's appraisal committee, and past codirector of Cushman & Wakefield's national appraisal division. (CHAPTER 10)

Cesar J. Chekijian is vice president of the corporate real estate group at Manufacturers Hanover Trust Company in New York. A graduate of the University of London in engineering, he holds the Master of Corporate Real Estate (MCR) designation from NACORE. He is also a member of the NACORE board. (CHAPTER 7)

James A. Chronley is senior vice president for development at Taco Bell Corporation, Irvine, California. A graduate of Brown University in economics, he has held senior real estate positions at ARCO, Marriott Corporation, and Burger Chef. Mr. Chronley holds the Master of Corporate Real Estate (MCR) designation from NACORE and is chairman of its board. (CHAPTER 6)

Neil O. Dahlmann is president of Dahlmann Properties Company, Highland Park, Illinois, and was formerly vice president of the healthcare facilities and real estate subsidiary of American Hospital Supply Corporation. He has written/edited several manuals on facilities development. A graduate of the University of Illinois in architecture and finance, he also holds the Master of Corporate Real Estate (MCR) designation from NACORE. (CHAPTER 1)

Sandford I. Gadient is president of Huntress Real Estate Executive Search, Inc., in Kansas City. Huntress was founded in 1971 and has become the nation's leading firm specializing in management consulting to the real estate industry in the areas of organization, compensation, and executive recruiting. He was an undergraduate at Arizona State University and received an MBA degree from the Wharton School of the University of Pennsylvania. (CHAPTER 5)

Bernard P. Giroux is vice president for marketing at Marathon U.S. Realties, Inc., and was formerly executive vice president of Montgomery Ward Properties Corporation. He earned a master's degree in real estate from the American University. Mr. Giroux is a fellow of the American Institute of Corporate Asset Management and a senior member of the Society of Appraisers. (CHAPTERS 10 AND 14)

Norman D. Holst is a vice president at Commerce Bancshares, Inc., in Kansas City. He has extensive experience as an economic consultant, an urban economist, and a public administrator. A graduate of the University of Missouri, Mr. Holst holds the Master of Corporate Real Estate designation from NACORE and has served on its board. (CHAPTER 9)

Ralph C. Hook, Jr., is professor and chairman of the marketing department and former dean of the College of Business Administration at the University of Hawaii. Dr. Hook is also a senior consultant for Huntress Real Estate Executive Search, Inc., in Kansas City and heads its research department. (CHAPTER 5)

Gerald M. Levy is senior vice president of the Real Estate and Corporate Services Division of Chemical Bank in New York. He has had management responsibility for construction lending, real estate finance, commercial banking, corporate real estate, and real estate consulting. Mr. Levy is a graduate of Columbia and Harvard Universities, a member of the American Institute of Real Estate Appraisers (MAI), a contributing editor of *The Real Estate Finance Journal,* and a director of the American Arbitration Association. (CHAPTERS 2 AND 4)

Elliott S. Matz is vice president at Chemical Bank in New York, responsible for long-range planning and asset development projects. He is a graduate of the University of Pennsylvania and the Harvard Business School. (CHAPTERS 2 AND 4)

Robert McLean, III, is senior vice president and development director at Cushman & Wakefield in Pittsburgh. (CHAPTER 12)

Ronald R. Richard is senior principal for management information systems in the accounting firm of Laventhol & Horwath, Chicago, Illinois. (CHAPTER 8)

Luigi Salvaneschi is senior vice president for real estate and construction at Kentucky Fried Chicken in Louisville and was formerly corporate vice president for real estate administration at McDonald's Corporation. He is a lawyer and a member of the NACORE board. (CHAPTER 3)

William J. Scarpino is a vice president at Collins Foods International, Inc. He holds an MBA degree and the Master of Corporate Real Estate designation (MCR) from NACORE. Mr. Scarpino is a past member of the NACORE board. (CHAPTER 11)

David P. Segal is vice president for corporate real estate at Dunkin' Donuts, Randolph, Massachusetts. He earned an MBA degree from Columbia University and is a graduate of the PMD program at the Harvard Business School. Mr. Segal holds the Master of Corporate Real Estate designation from NACORE, where he is a trustee and member of the board. (CHAPTER 13)

Robert J. Sule is a vice president at Cushman & Wakefield in Pittsburgh and was formerly real estate director for the Dravo Corporation. He is a former member of the NACORE board. (CHAPTER 12)

Preface

Corporate real estate—the land and buildings owned by companies not primarily in the real estate business—is an aspect of corporate affairs largely ignored in boardrooms across the country, despite the fact that real estate typically accounts for at least 25 percent of a company's assets. Most American firms do not clearly and consistently evaluate the performance of their real estate, treating it instead as an overhead cost like stationery and paper clips.

A principal reason for this is the lack of a standard work on the subject of corporate real estate, a problem this book is designed to solve. The sole purpose of this volume is to help those who deal with corporate real estate deal with it successfully in any or all of its aspects. For senior corporate real estate executives and the senior managers to whom the real estate unit reports, Section 1 offers eight essays that will help you understand, evaluate, and make better use of this asset. For junior practitioners, Section 2 offers a survey of how best to perform the six most common corporate real estate activities. For students and teachers of real estate, and business administration generally, the entire book provides a survey of this special area of practice.

Each contributor ranks among the most prominent people active in corporate real estate today. Drawing cases and examples from their own experience, they demonstrate why every company should, and how any company can, reconcile operating objectives with real estate opportunities to control costs and produce profits.

In addition to the contributors, who labored so hard to bring this book about, I owe special thanks to several others. Joseph R. Bagby, president and trustee chairman of NACORE, the International Association of Corporate Real Estate Executives, has encouraged and supported this undertaking from the very beginning. Esther B. Marshall, program director of NACORE's Institute for Corporate Real Estate, was most helpful in identifying and recruiting potential contributors. Finally, Joann Power provided invaluable assistance in preparation of the manuscript.

Robert A. Silverman

Corporate
Real Estate
Handbook

PART 1

Strategic Considerations

1

1

Determining Real Property Assets

Neil Dahlmann

President, Dahlmann Properties Company

In order for corporate management to make current decisions, to plan for the future of the company, and to take advantage of opportunities as they arise, a well-organized, up-to-date inventory of the company's real estate is needed. Such an inventory enables management to compare dollar values and bottom-line results location by location and provides a current, consolidated record of all owned and leased properties, thus helping management understand, evaluate, and make better use of the firm's real estate assets. With a focus on dollar impact and bottom-line comparisons, the executive summary reports of key ratios and indexes can facilitate management by exception and can provide senior management with additional data to determine which locations to keep or abandon and where and how to expand. A good real estate inventory and reporting system can be used effectively by senior management to motivate the real estate managers who will be evaluated by the system and will help everyone properly utilize the real property assets of the company.

Management's Need to Know

Data for Decisions

In making decisions that affect the future of the firm, management needs to be kept informed about constantly changing trends and must be able to sort out and focus on the key factors that will determine the company's ability to achieve, or even exceed, its goals. Executives need to give a sense of direction to employees, spot opportunities, and establish standards. Certain activity indexes, such as gross sales, cash flow, net income, and number of employees, can be compared with location-by-location statistics, square-foot ratios, and other data to help evaluate the needs and performance of a given location or a particular manager. The quality and location of the company's properties have a major impact on sales, profit margins, return on capital and equity, growth in net working assets, and cash flow.

The Real Estate Inventory as a Strategic Planning Tool

A well-organized real estate inventory enables senior executives to determine more effectively which operations or properties need their attention, and in which order. To produce a continually increasing stream of profits, executives need to instill a sense of urgency in their staffs, determine what to retain or abandon, and decide where and how to expand. The real estate inventory can answer many of these questions and thus form a basis for decisions that have a major dollar impact on the organization. It is a principal device for self-appraisal of the company's resources, strengths, weaknesses, and style. It also allows comparison with the firm's environment: the competition, the industry, and the economy. Management can use the inventory to perform a portfolio analysis of real property assets, and this can be integrated into the firm's strategic planning process.

Because it is easy for the real estate inventory document to become voluminous and unwieldy, it should have an executive summary that is concise, crisp, easily understood, and efficient in focusing on the key issues critical to management. It should also be recognized that there are limitations to the use of the company's real estate inventory: The environment may change and the data may not be suitable for solving current crises. Periodically updating the inventory could become just a ritual of putting numbers in boxes. The cost of an improperly managed inventory can outweigh the benefits.

Normally, the executive summary is the only portion of the inventory reporting system that is distributed to top management. All of the detailed statistics, plans, surveys, and documents should be readily available, if needed. If the entire inventory document is distributed, such a large statistical report runs the risk of being ignored by management. Even the executive summary must be simplified if senior management is to read and use it.

Lost Opportunities

In many companies, information about property is often gathered only when a firm is considering the sale, lease, or development of a particular location. The influence of real estate on everyday sales and operating costs or profits is often overlooked. Excess space means increased overhead costs; insufficient space means fragmentation of departments and increased handling costs. It is important, therefore, to determine exactly how much real estate is required for a given business to earn the greatest dollar return on its assets.

An example of a lost opportunity is the value of underlying land outgrowing the current use of a property. This often occurs when companies charge rent to their departments or transfer buildings to their divisions at figures based on the book value of properties rather than on current fair market value. One such firm established a regional warehouse operation in the heart of Silicon Valley long before the advance of the computer industry caused significant escalation in property values. The company could easily free up fixed-asset dollars and take a large profit by selling the property and moving the operation to a less valuable site. It is losing that opportunity, however, because the managers in the division have kept the operation where it is, not wishing to be charged for the cost of a new location but preferring the depreciated value of their current facility.

Purpose of a Real Estate Inventory

The Inventory as a Tool

A good inventory focuses on the dollar value and utility of the firm's real estate, providing estimates of fair market value for owned properties and comparable rent figures for leased properties, along with information about both book values and property tax values. Management can then use this data to:

- Charge fair market rent to individual departments and tenants
- Account for properties individually
- Apply sophisticated methods of investment analysis to each property

Purpose of Corporate Real Estate

The primary purpose of corporate real estate is to provide the land and buildings needed to carry out the company's business efficiently. Thus, the major questions influencing the real estate inventory are (1) How much space is needed? and (2) When does it have to be available? The answers must consider four fundamental factors:

- Future space needs
- Space available currently
- Lead time to acquire or dispose of space
- Space obsolescence

An operation can become a candidate for relocation owing to needed expansion or consolidation or to needed improvements. Because crowding beyond a certain point leads to inefficiency, expansion may be needed to provide adequate facilities for effective use of staff and operations. Consolidation may be indicated if the operations are spread too widely and have become inefficient or if changing business conditions create a need for the business to contract. On the other hand, the desire to improve the image and status of an operation can be a very important reason for a move because it can have a direct bearing on the ability to attract and keep competent employees. In trying to control operating costs, a company's real estate managers need to adopt an acceptable quality level (somewhere between "Taj Mahal" and "cheap city") based on the type of business and employee requirements. Productivity can be greatly affected by such factors as location, office design, job layout, lighting, temperature, ventilation, safety, music, and aesthetics.

When a Real Estate Inventory Is Needed

Most multilocation companies should maintain a consolidated, up-to-date, inventory of all their real estate—owned and leased. The exceptions may be firms that have only a few properties located in a single metropolitan area.

Precautions to Take with a Real Estate Inventory

80-20 Rule

In a typical company, management attention should be directed only to about 20 percent of the firm's locations at a time. The most important factor determining executive action is usually the dollar impact on the entire organization. Some of these properties will be performing significantly better than others, and senior management's objective will be to discern what leads to success, so it can be duplicated elsewhere. Another group of locations will be at the low end of performance, and the goal here will also be to learn why. Is the problem operational? Is it the location or the facility? The task is either to solve the problem or to abandon the location, if performance is chronically unacceptable, and to try to avoid this type of performance elsewhere.

Is the Inventory Itself Reasonably Accurate?

From time to time, the real estate inventory should be reviewed by management for commonsense logic. When a statistician is determining the number of square feet in a building, estimating fair market value, or comparing rent rates, misinformation or clerical errors can easily find their way into the inventory.

It is also important to make periodic spot comparisons of the records to verify proper functioning of the system. An example of a problem that went undiscovered for many years comes from a firm in the Midwest that has about 70 buildings, most of them on one large campus, some of them dating back to the early 1900s. On one part of the main campus three connected mid-rise buildings surround a large vacant site. Years ago the local property tax assessor, looking at a property map, thought the drawing showed a building where the vacant lot is and assessed it as a site with a building on it. The company, without an accurate real estate inventory for comparing their buildings with the property tax bills, paid taxes on this large, phantom facility for over 20 years.

Real Estate Inventory Formats

Inventory reports should comprise two categories: Certain information can be conveyed in periodic reports, while other data should be constantly available. All of the information should be presented in standard form in the various types of reports, and all of the reports should be in a simple format.

An efficient method for keeping the inventory is to place it on a personal computer. There are off-the-shelf software programs available that provide ease of maintenance and updating; allow sorting based on various items such as size, type, or location; maintain an updated list of "action dates;" and provide the needed reports.

Information for a Real Estate Inventory Report

Companies will require different inventory information, depending on their business activity and management needs. Generally, the following data should be included for each property. Some of the items, such as property values, rent rates, and the summary of bottom-line performance, should be stated in nominal figures and also compared to a standard, for example, on a square-foot basis.

Data for all facilities:

- Use

  - Existing use
  - Estimate of percent currently utilized
  - Possible better uses

- General description of site and improvements

- Size of building

- Amount of land

- Age

- Occupancy date

- Zoning

- Historical bottom-line performance

Data for owned facilities:

- Acquisition cost

- Capital improvements

- Estimate of current market value

- Capital needs

Data for leased facilities:

- Summary of lease terms

- Options to renew

- Options to purchase
- Leasehold improvements
- Estimate of current comparable rents
- Needed improvements

Additional Miscellaneous Data:

- Depreciation schedules
- Property tax bills and statements
- Maintenance and repair records
- Property deeds, easements, licenses, rights-of-way, title insurance, surveys
- Blueprints or floor plans
- Expansion space
- Leases
- Space allocation reports showing percent of utilization
- Mortgages
- Physical evaluation reports
- Long-range plans for facilities

Figures 1.1*a*, 1.1*b*, and 1.1*c* show sample forms and pages for corporate real estate inventory reports.

Standard Ways of Comparing Properties

Many companies have found it beneficial to prepare their own standard lease forms, standard contract documents, checklists for maintenance, and agreements for buying or developing new facilities. By using the same forms each time, with appropriate modifications to suit individual situations, the real estate unit and top management are more easily able to understand, monitor, control, compare, and report on the terms, conditions, options, and other factors affecting a large number of properties.

Square footage of floor area is one of the common denominators for comparing one location or department to another. Some of the more common ratios include cost of construction per square foot, rent per square foot, acquisition cost per square foot, current market value per square foot, sales per square foot, square feet per employee, square feet per quantity of output, and utilities expense per square foot. While square-foot ratios are very useful methods of comparison, there are several dif-

Bldg Id: _____   Bldg Purchase Date: _____   Bldg Land Sq Ft: _____
                                                        Bldg Land Acres: _____

Condition (D,V,D): ___   Date Disposed: _____
                          Selling Price: _____ $: ___(Type of Currency)

Building Address:
    Street: _____
    City: _____   State: _____
    Country: _____   Zip: _____
    Congressional District: _____

Owned (Y/N): ___Security (S,A,Both): ___   Title Ins on Bldg (Y/N): _____

Add a New Lease   Addlea
_____

Bldg Id: _____   Site Id: _____   Start Date: _____
                        Lease Type (G,N): ___   Finish Date: _____

Lessor Information:
    Lessor Name: _____
    Street: _____
    City: _____   State: _____
    Country: _____   Zip: _____
    Phone: _____
Mo Pymt: _____ $: ___ Index Incr: ___   Index Narr: (_____)
                  (Type of) (Y/N)   (_____)
                  (Currency)   (_____)
                                            (30 Character/Line)

Obligation (Y/N):
    Repair/Maint: ___   Comm Area Maint: ___   Ppty Tax: ___   Bldg Ins: ___

Add Occupant Information   Addocc
Bldg Id: _____   Division: _____   Headcount: _____
Vacancy Date: _____
Dimension Information (Sq Ft):
    Distribution: _____   Manufacturing: _____
    Office: _____   R & D: _____
Address Information:
    Street: _____
    City: _____   State: _____
    Country: _____   Zip: _____
    Phone: _____

Figure 1.1a. Inventory form. (American Hospital Supply Corporation, Evanston, IL.)

October 31, 1985   Inactive
Account: Ca-218   Lease # 7635   Tax ID #
Lessor: Continental Assurance Company
    Attn: Real Estate Dept.
    CNA Plaza, 41st Floor
    Chicago, IL 60685

Vendor Code: 001816289
Payee: Continental Assurance Company
    Attn: Cashier, Real Estate CA-37176
    CNA Plaza, 32ND Floor
    Chicago, IL 60685

Location: 5500 Union Pacific Avenue
    City of Commerce, CA
Rent: 7,794.00 mo   Lease Date: 06/30/67
Comments: Capital Lease
    Supersedes CA-217
    Cancelled 10/31/85

Facility: Warehouse
Facility Desc: 102,000 Sq. Ft.Whse.
Purpose: Office & Warehouse Space
Term: 08/25/67 to 08/24/87
Renewal:

Cancellation:

Taxes: Leg   Sublet:
Ins: Leg   Assigned:

Cancellation Penalty:
Lease Rev. Date: 08/86 - C
Action Deadline:

Lease Terminates: 10/31/85
Paid to: 11/30/85

Dept: M&L Chg:	Reason	Paid	Amount
1553-L7635	Rent	01/31/85	7,794.00
	Rent	02/28/85	7,794.00
	Rent	03/31/85	7,794.00
	Rent	04/30/85	7,794.00
	Rent	05/31/85	7,794.00
	Rent	06/30/85	7,794.00
	Rent	07/31/85	7,794.00
	Rent	08/31/85	7,794.00
	Rent	09/30/85	7,794.00
	Rent	10/31/85	7,794.00
			77,940.00

Barley Mill Plaza
Phips Mill Bldg.
Real Estate Division
Nancy McDaniel

Page 74

XDGSRE02 - PRTG091

Nov 11, 1985

Figure 1.1b. Lease summary. (E. I. du Pont de Nemours & Company, Inc., Wilmington, DE.)

ferent ways to calculate square footage, and it is important to understand which method is used in various situations. The methods for comparing operations within a company and in a real estate inventory report should be standardized. For everyone in the firm to understand the calculated ratios, it is important to use as few methods as possible for the various situations encountered.

Figure 1.2 shows three methods for measuring floor area. These methods are suggested by the American Institute of Architects (AIA) and the Building Owners and Managers Association (BOMA).

Property #3735

State	County	City	Plant
NC	Mecklenburg	Charlotte	

			Minerals
Dept(s)	Use	Easements	Reserved
		yes	

Total Acreage	Hazardous Waste Mgt.		
175.914			

Annie Lou Renfrow (widow) and Franklin MacMillan Renfrow (single) to E. I. du Pont de Nemours and Company
July 31, 1973 : $2,416,590 : 3609/0176 : Title Policy.
   366.15 acres of land lying between and being bounded by Monroe Road on the SW'ly side and East Independence Boulevard on the NE'ly side. Title was conveyed subject to easements granted to Southern Bell Telephone and Telegraph Company, Southern Public Utilities Company and Duke Power Company, as well as rights-of-way of Seaboard Coast Line Railroad, Old Monroe Road and East Independence Boulevard, and the rights of others to the uninterrupted flow of Ervin and McAlpine Creeks.
   This property was purchased by Du Pont with a cash payment of $483,318 with the balance of $1,933,272, secured by a note dated August 7, 1973, over a period of ten years payable in equal semiannual installments of $96,663.60 together with interest on the unpaid principal at 6 1/2 percent per annum. The first installment is due February 7, 1974.

E. I. du Pont de Nemours and Company to Family Dollar Stores, Inc.
August 18, 1976 : $78,269.00 :
   Conveys 6.806 acres being in the most S'ly portion of Du Pont Property 3735, bordered on the W. by Old Monroe Rd., on the E. by Seaboard Coastline Railroad, on the S. by other lands of grantee, and on N. by the lands of Pic 'N Pay Shoes (also conveyed this day by Du Pont).

E. I. du Pont de Nemours and Company to Pic 'N Pay Stores, Inc.
August 18, 1976 : $466,305.00 :
   Conveys 44.410 acres being S'ly portion of Du Pont land as lies between Old Monroe Rd. and The Seaboard Coastline Railroad. Land is bordered on S. by 6.806 acres owned by Family Dollar Stores, Inc. (as conveyed 8/18/76 from Du Pont, also).

E. I. du Pont de Nemours and Company to Pic 'N Pay Stores, Inc.
January 11, 1977 : No Charge :
   Correction deed—correcting that Pic 'N Pay is a corporation of Delaware not North Carolina as stated in deed of 8/18/76.

E. I. du Pont de Nemours and Company to the City of Charlotte
August 30, 1978 : $3,692 : 4123/0727:
   Easement for underground sanitary sewer or water lines (maximum of three (3) along and with two ways, each 25 ft. in width running along the entire

---

Figure 1.1c. Property printout. (E. I. du Pont de Nemours & Company, Wilmington, DE.)

W'ly side of Beards Creek and the S. side of Irvins Creek. Easement contains Abandonment clause.

E. I. du Pont de Nemours and Company to Duke Power Company
December 17, 1979 : $32,000 : 4268/707:
Easement for an electric transmission line situated along the N. side of the Seaboard Coastline Railroad running through the center of our property. Easement contains indemnity, relocation, and termination clauses.

E. I. du Pont de Nemours and Company to Sardis-Monroe Road Investors
May 25, 1982 : $2,000,000 :
139.02 acres being all the land from east to west between the Seaboard Coastline Railroad and Monroe Road and from north to south all land from Delmar Printing Co. to Pic'N Pay Shoes, Inc.

E. I. du Pont de Nemours and Company to Oatfield International N.V., a Netherlands Antilles Corporation
February 14, 1983: $2,500,00: 4627/0816: Title Policy
Conveys all of the above property.

Figure 1.1c. (Continued)

Types of Reports

If the real estate inventory is maintained as a computerized database, a variety of reports can be generated. Depending on management needs, a list of possible reports includes

- Executive report

    "Stars" and "dogs"
    Real estate department activity and results
- Various working reports

    Net book value
    Estimates of market value
    Leases due for review
    Statistics on leased property
    Leases by facility
    Leases by state
    Leases by operating division or department
    Leases by type of facility
    Facility type
    Facility location
    Leases due to terminate within the next___months
    Action deadlines
    Lessee/lessor names
    Property number
    Subleases

METHODS FOR MEASURING FLOOR AREA IN BUILDINGS

1. *Owned Facilities and Leasing Entire Buildings*

   cSF = *construction Square Feet.* The construction area method of measurement is used primarily for comparing building costs or values and is not used for leasing purposes, except where an entire building is leased to a single tenant.

   It is computed by measuring to the exterior faces of exterior walls or from the centerline of walls separating buildings. The construction area of a building is the sum of the construction area of all enclosed floors of the building, including basements, mezzanines, mechanical equipment floors, penthouses of headroom heights, columns, elevators, stairs, etc. The construction area does *not* include covered walkways, canopies, open plazas, open-roofed areas, pipe trenches with less than headroom height, exterior terraces or steps.

2. *Office Leases—Multitenant Floors*

   (a) uSF = *usable Square Feet.* Usable area is that portion of a floor or an office suite in which the tenant may put furniture and equipment for actual office use. It includes spaces that are dedicated to a single tenant's use, such as private bathrooms, private staircases, etc. Usable area is of prime interest to a tenant in evaluating the space offered by a landlord. The amount of usable area on a multitenant floor can vary over the life of a building as floors are remodeled and corridors changed.

   The usable area of an office is computed by measuring to the finished surface of the office side of corridor and other permanent walls, to the center of partitions that separate the office from adjoining usable areas, and to the inside finished surface of the dominant portion of the permanent outer building walls. It includes structural columns and projections. Usable area does *not* include public lobby and corridor space; public bathrooms; mechanical, electrical, telephone, and janitor's closets; elevators, stairs, and vertical ducts; their enclosing walls; and the thickness of exterior walls.

   (b) rSF = *rentable Square Feet.* The rentable area of a floor is the actual usable area plus common areas on that floor: public lobby and corridor space; public bathrooms; and mechanical, electrical, telephone, and janitor's closets. These shared, common areas usually add an additional 10% to 15% to the usable area. Rentable area measures a tenant's pro rata portion of the entire office floor, excluding elements of the building that penetrate through the floor to areas above or below. The rentable area of a floor is normally fixed for the life of a building and is not affected by changes in corridor size or configuration. Landlords generally use this method for quoting rent rates, for use in computing the tenant's pro rata share for rent escalation clauses, and for measuring the total income producing area of a building. On multitenant floors, the landlord should compute both the rentable and usable area for any specific office suite.

   The rentable area of a floor is computed by measuring to the inside finished surface of the dominant portion of the permanent outer building walls. It includes structural columns and projections. Rentable area does *not* include any major vertical penetrations serving multiple tenants: elevators, stairs, vertical ducts, etc.; their enclosing walls; and the thickness of exterior walls.

Figure 1.2. Methods for measuring floor area in buildings.
(Permission to reprint granted by BOMA International; copies are available for a fee from BOMA International Publications Department, 1250 Eye Street, NW, Suite 200, Washington, D.C. 20005.)

Lessee payments
Escalation clauses
Leases with renewal options
Leases with cancellation options
Lease termination dates
Sizes of facilities
Bottom-line performance
Capital improvements

Benefits of the Real Estate Inventory

With a concise, effective, well-organized, up-to-date inventory focused on the dollar value of the properties as well as on bottom-line results, senior management can take positive action to duplicate top performers, weed out problems, and know how the company's real estate is performing. The real estate inventory is also a major planning and control tool for the real estate unit to use in managing day-to-day corporate real estate activities. An effective real estate inventory motivates the real estate managers who are going to be evaluated by the system.

Up-to-date inventories thus protect the assets of the company. A current, effective real estate inventory helps prevent losses that could occur from selling property at below market prices or from making suboptimal investment decisions because of an incorrect assessment of costs or returns. A good real estate inventory can also facilitate both management by exception and management decentralization.

Most corporations are committed to providing the highest possible level of service to their customers. At the same time they have a responsibility to make sure the services or products provided are cost-effective. A company must carefully balance real estate costs with the desire to achieve customer satisfaction and bottom-line results. The ability to convey an understanding of actual real estate costs location by location is the major benefit of a good real estate inventory.

2

Choosing Strategic Objectives

Gerald M. Levy
Senior Vice President, Chemical Bank

Elliot S. Matz
Vice President, Chemical Bank

Corporate real estate is one of the most complex concerns of large-scale profit-making organizations; few functions are more important for the protection and enhancement of market share, efficient future expansion, and long-term financial results. Corporate real estate units must function at the crossroads of organizational life; the process by which decisions are made about future structures and strategies for specific operating business units is a difficult one. Despite the multifaceted environment in which corporate real estate managers operate, they must help achieve a consensus so they can fulfill their objectives.

Alternative corporate real estate concepts, opportunities and constraints of the corporate environment, and the range of available strategic real estate choices are examined here. Completion of a long-range real estate plan is important for acquiring an appropriate analytical database, highlighting possible strategic objectives, and providing an "education" for the senior officers of the corporation. The selection of strategic objectives should be one of the chief components of such a real estate plan, whose structure and main themes are proposed here.

Alternative Corporate Real Estate Concepts

There are three alternative concepts of corporate real estate activities:

Facilities Management Concept

Historically, the most common pattern has been a facilities management approach, which entails operating existing facilities, supervising the construction of new facilities, and buying, selling, and leasing properties as primary business needs change. Functions are often split among several dispersed units with different reporting lines. Even if a comprehensive facilities management unit exists, it generally is not coherently linked up to the mainstream strategic planning of the corporation as a whole and has no bottom-line emphasis. The relatively custodial and passive nature of this concept is often signaled by the assignment of retreaded personnel from the corporation's primary businesses. Generally, these corporate real estate officials have little or no meaningful prior experience in real estate or construction. Instead of exercising a high level of initiative, a unit so structured is generally reactive in nature.

Asset Management Concept

This more proactive approach is characterized by the deployment of professional real estate and construction personnel who utilize up-to-date managerial, financial, and real estate techniques to deliver and maintain relatively attractive physical facilities which are functional and economically sound. In the asset management mode, the corporate real estate unit will aim to achieve profits from time to time on a very limited risk basis and only in relation to situations when, in the past or present, the corporation had or has a requirement for partial or full occupancy of a property. A unit with an asset management focus generally has a wide range of activities situated in one relatively comprehensive corporate real estate organization.

Entrepreneurial Real Estate Concept

As in the asset management mode, an entrepreneurial real estate unit is staffed with sophisticated corporate real estate professionals, but it has a more comprehensive profit-making outlook and is generally willing to take a greater measure of risk to achieve its profit objectives. Satisfying the parent corporation's space requirements for its primary non-real-estate businesses is only one objective, and it often comes into conflict with the entrepreneurial entity's drive for profit maximization.

Which Concept to Choose

While a facilities management approach is rarely justifiable, not all corporations should automatically choose an entrepreneurial organizing concept for corporate real estate. Such a selection may cause a tug-of-war between the need to provide logistical and service delivery support for the ongoing operations of the corporation's primary non-real-estate businesses and the objective of achieving dramatic bottom-line profit results from real estate assets. For example, a foreign branch of an American financial services organization was relocated to a secondary location in relation to its primary business markets because the corporate real estate unit concluded that greater real estate value appreciation could be achieved at the new location. Diminution of profits in a primary corporate business may occur while real estate profits are enhanced.

In order to determine if an entrepreneurial approach to real estate is appropriate, one must compare the level of yields from investments in the corporation's primary businesses with those that can be realistically obtained from entrepreneurial real estate activities. The corporate leadership's receptivity to fairly significant risk levels and its ability to attract, compensate, and retain the highest caliber of corporate real estate managers are also key issues which must be resolved.

For many corporations, the asset management mode may prove to be the most practical and congenial. Although real estate profits are always to be encouraged, the need to service the corporation's primary businesses must often be given the highest priority. An alternative solution is an efficient corporate real estate organization with a primarily logistical and service focus and a separate, parallel entrepreneurial real estate entity.

Opportunities and Constraints of the Corporate Environment

The corporate culture—the formal and informal policies, attitudes, sanctioned behaviors, and approved methods for accomplishing objectives within a specific organization—presents special opportunities and constraints for corporate real estate officers. Such managers are affected by a series of conflicting requirements. They must deliver new projects and ongoing facilities management with a high level of quality, yet they must often meet corporate requirements for strenuous cost-control measures.

There is pressure in many corporations to standardize work environments in order to provide the employees of different business units with similar work amenities and also to promote flexibility in moving business units from one location to another within the corporation's space inventory with a minimum of incremental renovation costs. Many units are increasingly specialized in nature and their specific functional needs must be satisfied. Customizing layouts and still providing for maximum flexibility for future movement of business units at a minimum of cost is a great challenge.

Divisional managers or heads of subsidiaries, particularly those operating at a great distance from corporate headquarters, may believe in a do-it-yourself approach or may desire to bypass the internal corporate real estate unit in favor of an outside provider of services, whom they may easily control for parochial purposes. If overall real estate goals are to be systematically and effectively met, the chief corporate real estate officer must be vigilant, but tactful, to ensure that the centralized corporate real estate mandate is enforced.

Perhaps the greatest diplomatic challenge to corporate real estate managers is the process by which the location and scope of a proposed new business facility is formulated. This process often becomes the anvil on which the future business strategy of an operating business unit is forged. In this process there may be a lot of stops and starts until the operating business unit's managers and the corporation's senior policymakers reach a consensus as to the future direction of the unit's business.

Real estate and construction processes are often characterized by sudden crises and unforeseen problems within the highly cyclical and volatile real estate industry, but corporate real estate activities often occur in a large-scale organizational environment in which general management practices call for close monitoring of processes and the expectation of progressive quarterly results. The senior managers of the corporation, who are the monitors of corporate real estate results, are often most attuned to mass production methods or volume-service delivery processes. Such activities are characterized by a large volume of units produced in a fairly uniform fashion employing a highly formalized set of activities. A constant and precise set of monitoring activities leads to an "on-television" effect for corporate real estate managers. They must manage highly cyclical and volatile activities in an often risk-averse corporate environment.

Corporate real estate managers generally report to, and are judged by, senior officers who are not very familiar with the dynamics and pitfalls of real estate and construction. In the last analysis, the effectiveness of a firm's corporate real estate unit is judged by an informal senior-level public opinion poll. Credibility must be earned and must be carefully guarded.

Strategic Objectives: The Choices

Setting strategic objectives in corporate real estate involves resolving a series of healthy conflicts within the corporation while making appropriate choices among alternatives. Senior corporate managers must examine the conflicts in the context of their own organization before deciding on a strategic path.

Conflicts Which Lead to Choices

The most basic and natural conflict inherent in the corporate real estate function is the conflict between the desire for high-quality space and the need to restrict the level of capital expenditures. Typically, employees at all levels consider the quality of the space in which they work as a measure of their value to the corporation. The egos of managers are involved. It also can be argued that the performance of employees improves with the quality of the space in which they work. Managers desire high-quality, expensive space for themselves and their subordinates, yet senior managers often issue directives for lower capital spending. Concerned about improved income statement and balance-sheet ratios and about a lean image for shareholders, senior managers put pressure on the corporate real estate unit to hold down occupancy costs.

The effectiveness of corporate real estate managers may be measured by levels of rent and occupancy expenses (including amortization of capital expenditures) or by the satisfaction of the line managers who are the internal clients. The corporate real estate manager must balance the political problem of telling a line manager "no" against the policy committee's adverse perception of performance measured in terms of an increasing rent and occupancy expense line. The culture of each organization is unique, and every corporate real estate manager must arrive at a reconciliation of such counterforces.

As an example, consider Company A, which has Division X, which is in an autonomous business. Division X's managers requested that its location be separate from the rest of the corporation. They argued that the market share and profitability of the division's product line would improve if their workplace had an entrepreneurial image not linked to the parent corporation. Division X's managers requested that the corporate real estate unit fit out a separate high-quality building for the division's exclusive use. The corporate real estate unit wanted Division X to occupy vacant space in a building already leased by the corporation. The vacant space was available for sublet, but the market was soft, and there were no available outside tenants. Corporate real estate managers stated that the firm would benefit doubly if Division X occupied the existing vacant space by filling empty space already available within Company A's inventory and by avoiding the leasing of an additional facility. The trade-off facing senior corporate managers was the immeasurable dollar benefit of Division X's having an autonomous image versus the measurable dollar benefit of utilizing an underused corporate property. Division X was instructed to occupy the space which was vacant and already leased by Company A.

Related conflicts include the space allocation per employee and the number of private offices necessary in a unit's workplace. Those who are to occupy a space which is being constructed or renovated may believe that a generous allocation of space per employee and a high ratio of private offices will enhance morale and productivity. Others may state that more constricted space allocations and a lower ratio of private offices is more justifiable in economic terms. There is no one right answer for all circumstances. Morale and productivity must be served, yet capital costs and operating expenses must be held at reasonable and prudent levels.

A final major conflict involves the level of desirability of the location chosen for the facility. The managers of many business units wish to have their facility at a prime location. They often state that such a location is absolutely necessary for the fulfillment of their business objectives. Sometimes there is a masked or unmasked desire to be in, or close to, corporate headquarters so that managers may interface on a regular basis with the senior officers of the corporation, whom they seek to impress. Prime locations are necessary for certain business units; however, such locations should generally be avoided where the primary reason turns on egos, not profits. Locational alternatives and the major impact such choices have on rent levels have a substantial impact on rent and occupancy expenses.

Strategic Diversification Through a Varied Property Investment Portfolio

In assembling or managing a real estate portfolio in a risk-averse setting, it is useful to consider the necessity for control of particular properties over the long term and the goal of minimizing the growth of rent and occupancy expenses.

Sensitivity to control and to rent and occupancy expenses varies among corporations. For example, an investment banking firm may consider its image to clients extremely important and worth a very large investment in rent and occupancy expenses. Control of its premises over the long term is also of prime concern.

On the other hand, a chain of convenience stores may consider image to be less important, whereas the primary concern is low operating expenses. It may also require the ability to change the location of its outlets over time. Long-term control is, therefore, not as important.

Large diversified corporations have properties which fit into several categories of control and cost. For example, a large financial services firm may have a branch network that requires locational flexibility, but it may also have large headquarters and operations facilities which require control and efficient operating expenses.

By analyzing the control level of each major property, a corporate real estate manager can keep track of the whole portfolio and can be sure that the level of control is appropriate for the industry in which the corporation operates.

Real Estate Asset Matrix

To simplify the analysis, it is helpful to assemble a matrix of property control so that the corporate real estate executive can determine where on the control matrix each of the major properties lies and the direction in which each real estate asset is traveling (see Figure 2.1). (Note: the matrix assumes a stable or uptick real estate market.) The categories of properties on the matrix are

Cash Generators.   These are properties over which the corporation has a high level of control and which it has controlled for a long period. Typically, cost of occupancy for cash generators is low, and market value compared to book value is high. These are desirable properties for corporations which are locationally stable and are sensitive to rent and occupancy expenses.

High Potential Properties.   These are properties leased or purchased more recently and over which the corporation has a high level of control

	High control	Low control
Short-term control	High potential	Potential problem
Long-term control	Cash generator	Short fuse

Figure 2.1.

or where the corporation has an option for such a control level (purchase options and long-term fixed-rate renewal options at predetermined fixed-dollar amounts). Typically, while cost of occupancy is close to market levels, there is potential control of occupancy costs over the long term. These are desirable new acquisitions for corporations which are stable locationally and which are sensitive to rent and occupancy expenses.

Potential Problem Properties.   These are properties which are fairly recent acquisitions and over which the corporation has a low level of control (short-term leases, no options to purchase or renew). Typically, cost of occupancy is close to market levels. These are desirable properties for corporations requiring many small facilities which are locationally flexible and which require modest capital investments.

Short Fuses.   These are properties which have been controlled by the corporation for a fairly long period but over which the corporation is losing control because of expiring leases. Typically, cost of occupancy is low compared to market, but major capital expenditures will be required in the near term to replace the space. Cost of occupancy will revert to market in the near term. At one time these properties may have been desirable for the corporation which was unsure of its locational preferences. In general, these are now the least desirable properties.

Each corporation has unique business requirements. It also has its own ideal mix of properties for the control matrix. One should map out the present distribution of properties on the matrix and the ideal configuration. Subsequently, when opportunities arise to acquire or sell a property, the properties and the control mechanisms which help achieve an ideal control-matrix configuration can be selected.

Diversification Through Ownership, Leasing, and Staggered Options and Maturities

In the typical risk-averse corporation, the risk of exposure to the real estate markets is analogous to the risk of exposure to the financial markets. As one spreads risk of financial instrument maturities in the financial markets, so one can spread the risk of lease maturities in the real estate markets. Depending on one's opinions about future real estate market trends, lease maturities may be planned to take advantage of market upticks and declines. In a more risk-averse organization one may want to balance lease maturities.

For example, Company B has 300 retail locations, one headquarters property, and three manufacturing or back-office facilities. It has a lease

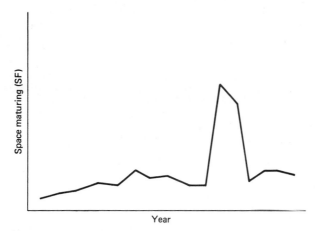

Figure 2.2.

maturity curve as shown in Figure 2.2. Retail leases are fairly evenly spread to mitigate market risk. Leases for major facilities, however, all mature during a two-year period, which causes great exposure in these years. In addition, the results of lease negotiations during this time period will affect the corporation for many subsequent years. If Company B is risk-averse, it may try to level out the maturity curve, as in Figure 2.3.

Similar studies and planning can be accomplished for the maturity of purchase options where factors include not only market risk but also a measure of the cost of internal capital. By drawing a curve of purchase option exercise dates, one can begin to manage the exercise of options. Company B's curve may look like the one shown in Figure 2.4.

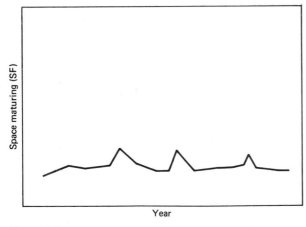

Figure 2.3.

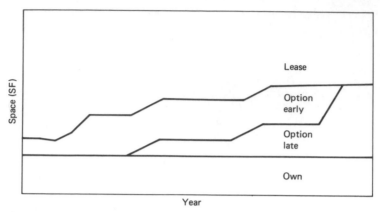

Figure 2.4.

Balancing leased, optioned, and owned properties on the matrix above may imply an ideal mix, as in Figure 2.5. The actual mix, Figure 2.6, may be different.

This process can identify leasing and acquisition strategies which will be useful in future negotiations.

Revenue Generation

In any sizable real estate portfolio there will be opportunities for asset development (realizing the value of an asset to the corporation) and revenue generation. Possible opportunities are described below.

Asset Development. Whether outsiders approach the corporate real estate executive or the corporation actively seeks outside interest, most real estate portfolios contain properties which can be more profitably developed. Asset development may include sale-leasebacks, sale of unused

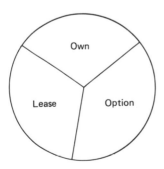

Figure 2.5.

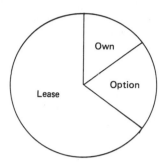

Figure 2.6.

air rights, disposal of surplus property, acquisition of investment property, and acquisition of property for future corporate use. All of these transactions may generate income which can offset rent and occupancy expenses or fund other capital investments. By reviewing the portfolio for leasehold advantages, air rights, and underutilized properties, the company can identify likely properties for revenue generation.

For example, Company C analyzed each of its leased properties for leasehold advantage (defined as the present value of the difference between market rent and the contract rent for the remaining term of the lease; fixed rental rate renewal options will often add to leasehold advantage). When the properties were ranked in descending order of leasehold advantage, the most likely candidates for sales of leasehold interests were pinpointed. Company C was able to sell several leaseholds and realize significant profits at certain locations when it moved operations to less expensive sites.

Entrepreneurial Activities. In reviewing the portfolio, a company may discover opportunities for riskier but more lucrative ventures. Joint venturing in the development of some of the company's properties could result in a higher return with greater accompanying risk. In order to determine the extent of recommended participation in high-risk ventures, the real estate executive working within a specific corporate culture must weigh regulatory issues, shareholders' priorities, the risk-taking posture of the company, and available opportunities.

Company D had an opportunity to sell its air rights over an old, existing facility in return for cash and equity participation in a residential condominium development next door. Senior management, inexperienced in real estate, was interested in equity participations, but the company was risk-averse. The corporate real estate unit opted for a minor equity participation in sales results in an uncertain market with a put and call, setting a floor and ceiling value for the equity, and with a major cash payment to the corporation for the remaining value of the air rights. In setting the cash payment, Company D carefully evaluated the potential cash results of the sales program. In this way, the risk of the deal was tailored to the character of the company and its management.

The Real Estate Plan Linked to the Corporation's Strategic Business Plan

Having reviewed the strategic choices, the corporate real estate manager can now begin to formulate the long-range real estate plan. To be effective, the real estate plan must start with an examination of the corporation's strategic business plan. Plans that are done in a vacuum, based on only real estate objectives, will conflict with the strategic business requirements of the firm. Plans done in conjunction with the corporate planning function can respond to broad needs of the organization as well as to real estate objectives. Because the strategic business plan is usually not explicit about real estate implications, additional input may be required, both from the strategic planning staff and from the line managers.

Organizing for Decision Making

The framework for a real estate plan should start with global issues. For example:

1. What is the mission of the corporate real estate function?
2. What overall guidelines govern corporate real estate decisions?
3. How much control is required in each real estate sector?
4. Is it preferable to lease or to own?

Based on the answers to these questions, overall guidelines can be set. Guidelines for a specific corporation might include the following:

1. The ideal owned/optioned/leased ratio must be balanced.
2. The curve of lease expirations must be flattened.
3. Keeping rent and occupancy expenses low may be more important than image in all but the headquarters portion of the real estate portfolio.
4. The ideal control matrix must concentrate all but headquarters facilities in the "potential problem" category. Headquarters facilities should be concentrated in the "high potential" category.

Using such overall guidelines, the real estate plan of a specific firm can now address individual issues for each of its sectors.

Real Estate by Organizational Sector

Within the corporate real estate portfolio are some facilities and locations which have similar characteristics. The portfolio can be divided into sectors within which the locations have similar real estate requirements. For example, retail facilities in Company E all require low capital investment, little long-term control, and, therefore, short leases and low ongoing rent and occupancy expenses. Similarly, properties in the manufacturing, warehousing, computer, back-office, headquarters, foreign, and sales-office sectors have their own real estate characteristics. Once the real estate portfolio has been sorted into sectors with common characteristics which can be related to the overall corporate strategic plan, future requirements by sector can be projected more accurately than forecasting for the portfolio as a whole.

Key Issues by Organizational Sector

In addition to its own real estate characteristics, each sector will have its own business strategy, which will dictate the overriding real estate issues. Such sector issues must be identified and their effect projected over the term of the real estate plan. For example, the management of the manufacturing sector of a high-technology company had a belief that a small plant environment promotes more efficiency in productivity levels than a very large one. Indeed, it was a corporate policy to have no more than 700 employees at any single manufacturing location. For this firm's corporate real estate unit, not only are location and labor markets important factors but growth and planning in maximum increments of 700-person facilities became an overriding issue.

Similarly, the headquarters staff of the same company had grown historically almost proportionally to the total growth in the number of company employees. Senior corporate management believed this was not necessary and arbitrarily decided that the headquarters facility would remain at its present size. Additional units which interacted with or supported headquarter functions, as well as the additional growth of units already existing within headquarters, had to be accommodated elsewhere. In planning for the headquarters sector, corporate real estate managers had to prepare for versatile and flexible satellite headquarters facilities to accommodate the evolving headquarters-related functions.

Supply-Demand/Quantitative Projections

To aid in specifying staff growth, the amount of space required, and rent and occupancy requirements, a systematic and quantitative projection method may be of use. With the help of a microcomputer and a spreadsheet program, simple projections of a large real estate portfolio can be generated and stored. Although there are several methods for producing real estate projections, the most common process includes (1) collection of data, (2) designing a model and generation of projections, (3) sensitivity analysis, and (4) evaluation.

Collection of Data.   Corporate real estate executives must approach line managers in each of the key corporate sectors for data on projected labor requirements, automation planning, locational requirements, and similar issues. Although such data projected by corporate managers over long periods are likely to be inaccurate, they are generally the only data available. In order to ensure that information received from various managers is comparable, standard definitions of growth trends can be used. For example, a manager may be asked whether the unit will experience growth through acquisitions (11 to 20 percent per year), major growth (7 to 10 percent per year), minor growth (3 to 6 percent per year), stability (no growth or decline), minor decline (3 to 6 percent per year), major decline (7 to 10 percent per year), or "shedding" (elimination or sale of unit). If the same definitions are used throughout the corporation, data from all the units can be projected and added up on a consistent basis.

Surprising and unusual predictions should be reviewed with the most senior managers of a firm, who may have a broader and more informed view of corporate strategy. In addition, overall projection figures should be checked statistically to be sure that projected real estate growth falls somewhere near the curve of historic growth. Although it is possible that the future may vary from the past, in large corporations it takes a major sea change in corporate strategy to cause a significant shift in an overall real estate growth curve.

Designing a Model and Generation of Projections.   Compounded growth projections and totals by unit, by division, and by sector with a corporate grand total can reveal surprising conclusions. Explosive growth in one sector may compensate for decline in another and can affect corporate real estate decisions. The model may also include staff projections and future rent and occupancy expense forecasts with an inflation adjuster. More sophisticated models can be purchased with software that allows for input of additional data, but the value of the incremental complexity is questionable.

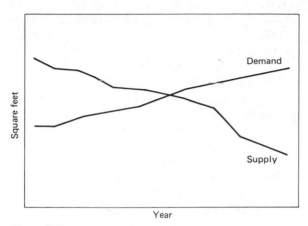

Figure 2.7.

Sensitivity Analysis.   Every projection should be reviewed for its sensitivity to each variable. For example, does a percentage point change in a division's growth projections significantly alter the 10-year figure? Does a small change in the area-per-person assumption change space requirements significantly? Such testing flags errors and problems in the projections. More important, sensitivity analysis can identify potential real estate problem areas for the corporate real estate executive.

Evaluation.   Projection of space demand coupled with present knowledge of space supply (owned facilities, lease expirations, options to purchase) can be used to create supply/demand graphs by unit, by division, by sector, and for the corporation as a whole. Analysis of the graphs can be useful in monitoring rent and occupancy expense growth and in projecting supply/demand crossovers (see Figure 2.7).

Additional computations can be performed by analyzing projected square feet per person, rent and occupancy expense per person, and other useful ratios. Analysis of the projections can be used as a tool in preparing the corporate real estate executive for problems and opportunities over the time span of the plan.

Comparative Financial Ratio Analysis and Objectives

Utilizing current data on one's own real estate and utilizing publicly available data on the real estate ratios of competing organizations, one can track the comparative real estate performance of the corporation. Although no two corporate strategic plans or real estate strategies are exactly alike, performance among competitors can be roughly compared and differences explained.

For example, a major bank which owns its headquarters facilities will probably have a lower-sloping rent and occupancy curve than one which leases such a core facility. A bank which has a branch system will have a rent and occupancy curve with a different slope from one which does not.

Simply being aware of a corporation's real estate situation in comparison to its competitors is important. Some corporations may see an advantage in setting goals based on their own performance as compared to the performance of competitors. By setting management objectives based on the average rent and occupancy performance of several competitors, senior management can ensure that the corporation does not fall too far from the norm on the rent and occupancy expense line of the corporate income statement.

The "Living Plan"— Computerized Sensitivity Analysis

In today's corporate environment, with senior managers often changing jobs, corporate strategies evolving, and mergers and acquisitions playing havoc with forecasts, the corporate real estate executive must be prepared to alter plans and projections at irregular intervals.

No plan is sacrosanct; indeed, no planning method is sacred. During every planning cycle, basic assumptions will change, perhaps requiring that the planning model or method change. If the planning model is computerized, not only can projections be tested for their sensitivity to changes in variables but basic assumptions and methods can be altered easily.

Conclusion

Choosing the strategic objectives which are to be given highest priority for a specific firm is highly dependent on its corporate culture, the strength of the firm's capital base and income tax position, the level of profitability of its primary business activities (with attendant opportunity cost considerations), the structure of its industry and its major competitors, and the degree of public regulation to which the corporation is subject. Some of these factors may diminish a firm's corporate real estate playing field.

3

Selecting Areas of Real Estate Activity

Luigi Salvaneschi

*Senior Vice President of Real Estate and Construction,
Kentucky Fried Chicken*

Real Estate Activities in General

The activity of a real estate unit is dictated by the nature of the company's operations. For a utility company, it may be acquiring or disposing of rights-of-way; for a paper firm, it may be the acquisition of forestry land and easements; for a railroad, it may be the establishment of storage, the acquisition of rights-of-way, or the disposal and development of properties; for a bank, it may be the acquisition and leasing of land in order to establish branches or electronic banking stations; for a retail company, it may be the acquisition of outlets.

From time to time, the main activities of a real estate unit may change, depending upon corporate needs. If the company is in a development stage, particularly if it performs repetitive development, the activity of the real estate unit will be geared to expansion. If the company elects not to expand but to consolidate its position, to increase its efficiency and productivity, the real estate group could be involved in the disposal of unusable assets and improving the returns of remaining properties. Not long ago, the oil companies were growing quickly, looking for service station locations. Then, because of the oil glut, retrenchment took place and their main real estate activity became the disposal or the development of many locations.

During the last few years, the attention of management has turned more toward corporate real estate assets. Traditionally, real estate was considered a means to an end—an asset subordinate to the company's principal business. Many companies have built up large real estate holdings, often worth millions. Now, there is a general reconsideration of those assets. It is part of a new productivity awareness in American business. Real estate assets are being looked at as potential income producers through sale, lease, development, or just better management. Facilities which have been producing losses for a long time are being transformed into sources of revenue.

There are six basic corporate real estate activities: acquisition, development, divestiture, property management, reacquisition, and support activities.

Acquisition of Facilities by Purchase or Lease

In any corporate real estate acquisition, the involvement of the real estate unit is advisable. Top management should not rely exclusively on brokers, developers, or other corporate officers. Operations executives might look at it from one standpoint, construction executives from another, and marketing executives from yet another, but, in the end, the real estate executive should weigh every element of the proposed acquisition to create a consensus, coordinating activities with other departments, outlining an action plan and a critical path. Additionally, the real estate executive has the responsibility of implementing the corporate strategy for purchasing or leasing the real estate in question.

The primary corporate real estate activity is the procurement of space for the company's own use. The company might have a policy of buying or of leasing space. It might do both. Facilities might already exist or they might be built to suit new company activities. Real estate personnel involved in such procurement must work with the facilities planning people to understand space requirements, amenities, and special needs, for example, research, development, or training.

Corporate space procurement typically requires the following 10 steps:

1. Review of current and planned space needs
2. Review of business plans and conformance with staff and space needs
3. Identification of potential locations

4. In-depth financial analysis of all options

5. Recommendation to management

6. Upon approval, detailed analysis of location and site selection

7. Design and construction

8. Concurrent with construction, planning department relocations, staff issues, equipment orders

9. Planning the disposition of existing buildings

10. Moves

Looking for office space in different cities for various regional branches presents a special challenge. Some companies retain the services of well-known property management companies that have professional contacts and offices in different cities.

There are two schools of thought about acquisition: Maximize the corporate cash flow by leasing, or purchase the fee and build up equity. The acquisition of excellent properties with multiple potential is the better way to go. Good real estate was created once. Additionally, greater equity will lead to greater and better borrowing capacity. In all real estate investments, one should look for a balance of real appreciation, equity, tax shelter, and cash flow.

Corporate Business Acquisitions

Recently, the acquisition and merger fever has struck many companies. Acquisitions and mergers may be part of strategic planning or may be caused by more immediate financial considerations. *The Wall Street Journal* is full of stories about successful and unsuccessful acquisitions. The acquisition of Kentucky Fried Chicken by R. J. Reynolds, for instance, was considered successful, while the acquisition of Jack-in-the-Box by Purina was not.

The involvement of the corporate real estate unit in corporate acquisitions and mergers has been less than it should be because corporate officers often do not grasp the importance of real estate holdings as part of the total assets of an acquisition or merger target. Real estate assets could produce large profits or big losses. Today's valuable real estate asset may disappear tomorrow if a lease expires. It might be perfect for one anticipated use and not zoned for another. The asset may look usable and yet it may have deteriorated. The present rent might be low but future escalations could be burdensome. Its location might be ideal for the present function but might be unsuitable for the planned function. Concealed encumbrances might make the asset far less desirable than what was reflected in the acquisition or merger assumptions. Certain assets acquired, moreover, may be of no value to the acquiring company, and they will have to be divested. A diligent examination of book values and market-user potential will be required. A loss of revenues from the disposal of the properties will have to be outlined by the real estate unit. Such problems will affect the economics of the total acquisition.

The corporate real estate executive can play a vital role in such acquisitions or mergers. It requires money, time, and human resources. It is up to the corporate real estate executive to be aware of the company's acquisition activities, to insert a real estate assessment into the process, and to demonstrate the benefit of such an assessment.

Development of Real Estate Assets

If a company intends to be in the development business, the real estate unit should contain development specialization and experience in-house. A railroad, for example, may own a large tract of land which could become the site of a regional shopping center, a factory, or a railroad yard. A retail company may own a parcel of land next to one of its outlets which would be ideal for a hotel.

Development opportunities are so diverse, requiring experience in various real estate fields, that analyzing them might strain the real estate unit. A warehouse, an office building, a shopping center, or a hotel would be developed differently. The real estate group most likely does not include such diversified development experience. Particularly today, specialization in these fields is critical. The financial penalty for inexperience may be in the millions. The use of outside consultants in the planning, designing, financing, and constructing of development projects is advisable.

Temporary Divestiture: Leasing and Subleasing of Real Estate Assets

Leasing and subleasing properties is a way to buy time in a period of uncertainty or to wait for a certain real estate event to happen which will enhance the value of the asset. A temporary divestiture might also be required by the tax earnings situation of the company. The decision, in this case, might be driven by financial requirements.

Leasing and subleasing are the easiest ways to recapture the value of a property. Negotiations of long-term leases should always contain the right to sublease without restrictions. Too many events might occur during the 20 to 40 years of a lease term that could require subleasing to protect the corporation from substantial losses.

Permanent Divestiture of Real Estate Assets

Permanent divestiture of real estate means the elimination of properties from inventory, often of properties that have been carried on the books for a long time. Individual divestitures need to be coordinated carefully with the firm's financial departments because they should occur at certain times during the operating year. Some divestitures involve substantial write-offs which could negatively affect the quarterly and yearly earnings. Such divestitures, therefore, must be scheduled correctly, and they must close in certain periods of the fiscal year. Most companies cannot afford to write off many large assets at the same time, even though the firm may have set aside reserves to cover such losses.

Divestitures may be connected with the relocation of facilities. A bank, for instance, might decide to close its branch in the center of town and open a new facility in a suburban shopping center. The acquisition of a new facility and the divestiture of the existing one require considerable cooperation between the real estate people involved in the different facets of the relocation.

The permanent disposal of assets through sale produces revenues that can be used for attaining the primary goals of the corporation. It is money that does not have to be borrowed. Leasing of assets demands they be managed. Records have to be kept and updated, rents have to be collected, property taxes must be analyzed, maintenance and repairs must be performed. The sale of assets, therefore, is preferable to a lease, unless the company is willing to be serious about property management.

Property Management

Proper real estate management is a sophisticated activity. Ideally, the property management function should be separate and distinct, with no involvement in other corporate real estate activities, although the property manager should report to the chief real estate executive.

Depending on corporate activities, real estate assets that might become part of the corporate inventory could include offices, plants and factories, storage facilities and warehouses, properties vacated due to cessation of business, properties acquired in corporate acquisitions, or properties acquired but never developed, rebuilt, or remodeled.

Property management requires accurate records of property characteristics, tenants, lease terms, and income and expenses. Such records demand regular monitoring. Detailed procedures should be in place concerning repairs, safety, security, contract services, and utilities. Property managers continuously review this management information. Annual budgets must be drafted, policies and procedures established, and each project separately evaluated against the operating plan. Special projects, like energy retrofits, are also implemented by property managers.

For a large company, a problem might be created by the dispersal of properties throughout the United States, perhaps internationally. The management of such dispersed real estate is most demanding and complex. Real estate managers must work closely with the construction department to keep the premises in usable condition, with the legal department to deal with tenant issues, with the accounting department to deal with receivables, and with real estate brokers to produce tenants. When corporate properties number in the hundreds or the thousands, the managerial specialization required does not allow most real estate departments to do the job properly in-house. Outside management companies are retained whose performance requires proper monitoring by the corporate real estate executive.

Real Estate Reacquisition

If a company leases a facility, it may become necessary to negotiate an extension of the lease or to buy the property. This activity is called *real estate reacquisition*. The timing of the negotiations is critical. If one waits until the last year before the expiration of a lease, one's negotiation power is curtailed and it may not be possible to get a longer term or more options under acceptable conditions. Once the company's strategic plan calls for remaining in a given location, renegotiation activity should be scheduled immediately. There are different thoughts about how many years ahead of lease expiration new deals should be negotiated. Much depends upon the time horizon of the tenant company. If renegotiations begin six to eight years in advance, the landlord must decide whether to continue under the present terms for six to eight years more or to improve terms in exchange for a longer lease, a purchase option, or something else of value to the tenant. The tenant must make a similar evaluation.

While in the search for a new site there might be several alternatives in the same area, there are no alternatives if the present business is prosperous and the company wants to stay in that location. The real estate negotiator, therefore, should contact the owner well ahead of lease expiration time and avoid the constraint of an impending deadline. Otherwise, the negotiating position would be extremely weak and might lead to very unfavorable renewal terms for the tenant company.

The activity of the reacquisition representative, therefore, is substantially different in nature from the activity of a new acquisition representative. It requires another style of negotiating. One deals only with the individual who owns the property where the company leases the facility. Because the option for alternate sites does not exist, the negotiations require steadiness, strength, patience, and persistence. Impatience and undue pressure are counterproductive in the reacquisition activity.

The reacquisition function should have its own policies and practices. They involve the calculation of the present values of the future rents, the residual value of the real estate, and the market and economic evaluation of the property, as well as future financial projections. Not only should leases be reviewed and renegotiated, if necessary, but survey problems, easements, title encumbrances, and the like should be cleaned up.

Support Activities

Real Estate Financing

The role that the real estate executive should play in corporate strategic planning and, consequently, in the setting of budget goals has already been suggested. These functions require allocation of capital. The capital required for real estate is a function of the real estate activity planned in the budget. The dialogue between the chief real estate executive and the chief financial planner must be open, articulate, and detailed. No corporation can run the risk of having the financial executive come up with assumptions that are not validated by the real estate plan. Additionally, real estate situations might not be in step with the financial pace. Financial assumptions, for instance, might anticipate revenue from the disposal of a warehouse by June 1, but the warehouse might have been condemned by the fire department and scheduled to be demolished on August 1. Financial assumptions must be reconciled with real estate facts.

Real estate and finance units should allow each other a degree of flexibility because real estate is such a fluid activity. Real estate units review their goals for the coming budget year and work out a series of contingency plans with the financial unit. Special attention should be paid to accounting policies and procedures so they can be modified to fit real estate activities. Policies and procedures should not hamper or delay the flow of real estate events.

Real Estate Law

Corporate attorneys are an essential part of real estate activity. Consequently, a question arises about whether real estate attorneys should be part of the corporate real estate unit or the law department. The decision-making process involving field representatives, management, and real estate attorneys is better served if the attorneys are part of the real estate organization. Also, when real estate legal support is in-house, attorneys have a better understanding of the many facets of corporate real estate activities, which enables them to better protect the company. The real estate legal group must protect the company's interests without stifling creativity. This means finding more reasons to make a deal than to kill it. When the real estate lawyers are a part of the corporate real estate department, this is more likely to occur. The attorneys may then report in a staff relationship to the corporate chief counsel. The correct number of attorneys must be directly proportional to the plan of the real estate unit and the long-range plan of the company. There is no point in forecasting a determined number of deals if real estate legal support is lacking.

Real estate legal activities are dictated by company needs. A company, for instance, might be in need of financing. Real estate lawyers, therefore, will be directed to deal with lenders. Title reports will be carefully scrutinized for covenants, conditions, and restrictions of title, easements, and other encumbrances because the lender will require a clean title. In addition, the company itself might be particularly concerned about certain rights—for instance, the right to sublease the property, free usage of premises, special clauses concerning structural maintenance and repairs, or protection for corporate tenants.

Another important activity of the real estate legal group is real estate litigation. There is no large company without a list of pending cases. This requires more internal activity as well as retaining outside counsel. Outside counsel requires instruction, direction, and supervision, a time-consuming job for in-house real estate attorneys. The senior real estate executive should continuously monitor the litigation list, analyze the causes, and take appropriate steps to minimize litigation.

The real estate executive should work with senior management and the chief counsel to establish a list of legal standards by which all transactions will be regulated. These standards give a powerful negotiating tool to real estate field representatives, and they are essential for obtaining clean agreements and protecting company rights.

Additional Support Activities

Depending on its principal real estate activities, each company has a need for specialized real estate services. A lending institution, for instance, will need appraisers for properties which are candidates for financing. From time to time, all large companies must deal with condemnation proceedings, for which specialists will be required. Other companies leverage their real estate assets through tax-free exchanges. This field is extremely technical. Investment companies might need real estate syndication experts. The development of apartment complexes requires the services of experts in organizing condominiums and cooperatives. Because of the growing regulatory environment in many communities, zoning, environmental, or historical preservation specialists may be needed to deal with local citizens as well as public officials.

The relocation of employees, too, is a normal occurrence in many firms. A company may have people who develop contacts with local brokers for the purchase and sale of homes. Sometimes, outside real estate firms are engaged. The inventory of unsold employee homes may become substantial, losses may accumulate rapidly. Relocation, therefore, can be a production function, which requires an active staff. Real estate attorneys may also be assigned to support the home sale activities.

This list of specialists gives an idea of many real estate activities, direct or indirect, that may be part of the corporate real estate function.

Conclusion

The typical corporate real estate unit deals with millions of dollars in company assets. The importance of this function is such that it affects the strategic plan. The dialogue between the senior real estate executive and other strategic planning executives should be open and constant. The corporate real estate executive is often in a unique position for understanding all implications of any real estate decision, a position of total business responsibility.

4

Implementing Strategic Objectives

Gerald M. Levy
Senior Vice President, Chemical Bank

Elliot S. Matz
Vice President, Chemical Bank

Once strategic objectives have been chosen, there are a number of management and real estate techniques which are important in providing effective and coherent performance in specific situations.

Management Techniques

Consensus Building for Specific Capital Project Decisions

At the initial stages of a proposed capital project, officials of the corporate real estate unit meet for preliminary discussion with the senior managers of the division requesting a new facility or the renovation or expansion of an existing workplace. Appropriate fieldwork, interviews, and analytical work are completed by corporate real estate personnel. Once it is certain that all managerial and financial guidelines have been met, with some possible noted exceptions for subsequent resolution, a proposed project plan of action with accompanying proposed budget is tentatively agreed upon by both the client division's managers and senior corporate real estate executives.

Generally, major projects will require the approval of the corporation's policy committee. Doing one's homework and painstakingly building a consensus will generate a more impressive and effective presentation and increase the chances for a project approval from the policy committee. A constituency-sensitive building-block process is generally most appropriate, for example:

1. The head of the corporate real estate unit and the client division's general manager meet with the corporate controller. The proposed project concept and its budgetary implications are presented. The corporate controller is asked to identify any accounting, financial, legal, income tax, and regulatory concerns and questions. The chief corporate real estate officer and the client division's general manager answer some of the controller's questions. The task of researching the answers to the remaining questions is allocated to each of the logical officers within the corporation, and these questions are subsequently answered to the corporate controller's satisfaction.

2. The corporate controller, the chief corporate real estate officer, and the client division's general manager meet with the corporation's chief financial officer (CFO), who is also given a project presentation and a review of budgetary implications. At this meeting the CFO learns of the controller's review and acceptance of the project from a compliance point of view. Generally, the CFO will ask some additional questions, which, it is hoped, will be answered satisfactorily. If the CFO has confidence in the corporate controller's due diligence and believes that the proposal meets general policy guidelines, the project will most likely be endorsed.

3. The chief human resources officer is informed that project planning and budgeting has been coordinated with the appropriate experts and that all key questions about labor supply, wage and benefit issues, working conditions, industrial relations, and other relevant concerns have been satisfied. Generally, after asking some additional questions, the chief human resources officer will be satisfied and comfortable with the project and will endorse it from a technical viewpoint.

4. Other policy committee members whose sectors of managerial responsibility will be affected or who are likely to have a special interest in the proposed project are also given individual briefings and, it is hoped, will buy in during the process.

Although the outlined steps may vary in sequence and in the specific participants involved, depending on the hierarchical structure of a specific corporation, the objectives are always similar. The purposes of the process are to examine and resolve systematically and comprehensively all relevant issues and to build a consensus prior to the policy committee presentation. Individual preapprovals can be obtained by meeting with and satisfying all senior officials who are the repositories of the accepted corporate wisdom about the various technical issues which surround the project. Accordingly, the project is unlikely to be vetoed on technical grounds at the subsequent policy committee meeting. Similarly, all other corporate senior officer constituents who may have a special interest in the project have also been briefed and have had their concerns satisfied before the policy committee meeting. This consensus-building approach greatly improves the chances for a successful policy committee presentation.

Dynamics of Project Team Building

Any major corporate real estate project is complex and involves the intricate mobilization of labor, material, capital, and management to achieve project objectives. Each project process is necessarily embedded in the power relationships and often conflicting goals of different corporate managers. Substantial potential exists for visible mistakes, foul-ups, and bad results. Understandably, there may be an initial wariness among the key players involved in a proposed project effort. As a result of the "on-television" syndrome described in Chapter 2, all parties involved—whether they be from the internal client group, from the corporate real estate unit, or from other groups which interface during the project—are concerned lest they be blamed by senior management for problems which may develop.

Often risk transference is employed as a compensating tactic. One corporate real estate chief is fond of relating the story about a first meeting called by a divisional general manager and his aide in order to discuss the completion of a project. The complex and highly sensitive project had to be executed with extreme care and timeliness so that there would be no disastrous interruption of one of the corporation's core activities, which was essential for its very survival. The divisional general manager and the aide who was designated to coordinate activities with the corporate real estate unit each possessed an agenda outline, which they *did not show* to the chief corporate real estate officer, even after he requested a copy! After about ten minutes of dialogue, it was clear to the corporate real estate executive that the meeting was being structured in deliberate fashion, with note-taking as a protective device. If anything subsequently went wrong with the project, the divisional general manager would likely single out the chief corporate real estate officer for blame.

If these interpersonal dynamics were permitted to continue, the chances of a project failure would be greatly increased because the quality of inputs and the level of cooperation would be adversely affected by the climate of wariness. Although outranked by the divisional general manager of the internal client group, the head of the corporate real estate unit interrupted the unconstructive dialogue and made the following statement in an avuncular manner: "Gentlemen, it is clear to me that one of your main concerns is your fear of getting blamed if anything goes wrong with this project. I can assure you that if it fails we will all be blamed. I believe that in the interest of the corporation and in our own individual self-interests we should all stop expending time figuring out how to criticize the other fellow. Instead, I would suggest that we do our utmost to cooperate fully with each other so that the project will have the maximum opportunity of being completed on time and within budget; in this way we will all properly fulfill our duties to the corporation and everyone will appropriately bask in the glow of success. After all, we're really not on different sides of the table but on the same side—don't we all work for the same corporation?" After a period of awkward silence, the tension was broken and the participants went forward in an atmosphere of improved cooperation, and the project was successfully completed.

At the core of effective project team building is the need for open and honest communication, a high quality of inputs, comprehensive and harmonious coordination of the efforts of all participants, and the wide distribution of credit for a job well done. Participative management and a nonalienating consensus-building style will generally provide the best opportunity to create the desired conditions for successful project execution.

Managerial Accounting as a Strategic Control Device

A key issue in management accounting is the basis for allocating rent and occupancy expenses to each strategic business unit (SBU). Should rent and occupancy expenses be allocated on the basis of current external market rent levels or of prior contractual commitments which generally lag behind current open-market conditions?

The arguments in favor of market rate allocations are these:

1. If contractual rates are charged, divisional and corporate senior management will not necessarily perceive the masking effect of currently unrepresentative contractual rental rates still in effect and will generally be oblivious to the significant future negative impact on a unit's profitability at the point of lease renewal.

2. Charging market rates will discourage arbitrary space hoarding by a unit which may have only a vague possibility of usefully employing the surplus space in the near future.

3. Allocations based on market rates provide a "profit incentive" to the corporate real estate unit and strengthen its motivation to structure real estate transactions which are economically advantageous to the corporation, as compared with more conventional arrangements.

The arguments in favor of contract-rate allocations are as follows:

1. Contract-rate allocations are advantages that should not be denied to specific units. Most corporations are likely to have contractual advantages for some of their space at all times. To charge market rates may cause product pricing changes which will make a product line uncompetitive at the present time instead of at the future point of lease renewal. To charge market rates is to deny the corporation a stream of substantial current profits for the sake of a highly theoretical market-rate charge.

2. Since the corporation is already committed to numerous lease agreements, closing specific units which do not make a profit on a market-rent-rate-expense-charge basis only results in spreading the same aggregate level of rent and occupancy expenses over a smaller number of SBUs.

3. While some of the space vacated because of the elimination of theoretically unprofitable businesses could be sublet or assigned to other tenants over time, it is a lagging solution which still results in the interim spreading of rent and occupancy expenses over a smaller number of product lines.

There is no perfect answer which resolves for all time the market-rate versus contract-rate expense allocation controversy. Perhaps, the best solution is a dual-tracking system which can clearly show a business unit's current performance and long-term prospects.

A related controversy may be designated as the "luck of the draw" versus a pool-rate expense allocation system. Why should some units, lucky enough to be assigned contractually cheap space, receive an advantage over other units with the misfortune of being assigned contractually expensive space? If none of the affected units need better located or higher-quality space, why should they not be charged rent and occupancy expenses at the same rate? A common solution to this problem is to set up a pool-rate expense allocation method. For example, the "Greenfields Pool" might consist of all utilized office buildings in suburban locations which are within a 50-mile radius of New York City.

Another expense allocation problem involves the management accounting treatment of expenses incurred to carry vacant space. In periods of cost cutting, certain business units will quickly give up vacant and discretionary space or move to a cheaper location so that they can reduce the level of rent and occupancy expenses they are charged, yet the aggregate effect on the corporation as a whole may remain unchanged.

From a senior management point of view, it is useful to have a centralized inventory and expense tracking system to measure the expense impact of vacant space, so that appropriate action can be initiated to reduce the unnecessary inventory of excess space. Managerially, the corporate real estate unit should be charged with the responsibility of disposing of surplus space; for a certain period of time, however, the unit which gave up the space should continue to be charged for it for management accounting purposes. In this fashion, arbitrary and parochial actions in the acquisition or disposal of space are discouraged, while there is no delay in taking action to reduce the vacant space inventory.

Our discussion of these expense allocation controversies illustrates how management accounting can be used to discourage narrow-minded and economically dysfunctional behavior for the corporation as a whole and encourage an appropriately broad corporate perspective for divisional managers.

Centralized Capital Expenditure and Rent and Occupancy Expense Budgeting as a Managerial and Financial Discipline

The large aggregate of dollars to be spent and the long-term financial commitment involved in a major real estate project decision generally receives the attention and decision-making input of the senior officers of the corporation. Yet it is common for many projects to be initiated by divisional general managers, who are very knowledgeable about their product lines and have strong opinions about the size, scope, quality, and functional aspects involved in the delivery of proposed new facilities. Divisional managers are advocates for their specific needs and may lack an objective view of corporate priorities and broad corporatewide trends in capital expenditures and operating expenses. If corporate real estate project decisions are left almost entirely to the various line and staff divisions, the ad hoc and incremental nature of decentralized project decision making can have a devastating long-term effect on the corporation's overall expense structure and capital position. The unprioritized incremental growth of leasehold improvement amortization charges, furniture and equipment depreciation, rent payments, and other occupancy expenses can be a significant drain on corporate earnings. Since rent and occupancy expenses are in aggregate amounts generally second only to labor expenses in many firms, the negative impact on earnings can be very serious indeed.

The proper balance in project decision making is to have reasoned inputs and conclusions from divisional managers and policy committee members. The corporate real estate unit should recommend appropriate project solutions within overall corporate real estate resource allocation priorities. It should also have a senior level mandate to monitor approved policies and to aid in setting priorities through impartial analytical work. By instituting a centralized oversight and approval process in a corporation's annual profit planning cycle, the corporate real estate unit, working with the finance division and the senior officials of the corporation, can help reverse undesirable trends in rent and occupancy expenses.

Ideally, the corporate real estate unit's mandate should be sanctioned by the policy committee and communicated to all divisional decision makers. The mandate should call for the application of corporationwide criteria to all real estate projects initiated by the various divisions. This mandate will aid in long-term rent and occupancy expense rationalization and control.

Real Estate Techniques

There are numerous real estate techniques which can be utilized to help achieve chosen strategic objectives. Because these real estate concepts are highly variable and complex in their application, our review of each of them must, except for leasing, take the form of a brief summary highlighting a number of core issues.

Leasing

Because other real estate alternatives can be measured against the leasing concept, we must clearly understand the effects of leasing before we can evaluate other possibilities.

Landlords and real estate brokers often counsel corporations that space leasing is the preferred form of real estate activity for a firm whose major activities are not real estate in nature. With space leasing, capital may be preserved for investment in the corporation's primary business activities. This advice is sometimes, but not always, correct.

The pattern of rent payments made by tenants under the terms of space-lease agreements may be level rents for the life of the lease or they may exhibit a step-up or step-down rent schedule. Rent payments may be composed of a minimum guaranteed rent against an overage on sales, or in rarer instances, the rent may be completely calculated as a percentage of the tenant's sales at the leased premises. Sometimes, rents are adjusted at various times for a fractional or full relationship of the percentage increase in the consumer price or wholesale price indexes. The rent pattern negotiated in an individual situation is usually dependent on specific business circumstances, local custom, the amount of available space in the local or regional marketplace, and the respective ingenuity of the landlord and the tenant.

The gross lease and the net lease are two common arrangements. In the gross lease it is common for a tenant to agree to rent for its own use a portion of a multitenanted office building, industrial facility, or shopping center at a specific base rent. The landlord is generally responsible for property taxes and operating expenses up to a specific base "dollar stop," or the landlord's payment responsibilities are defined in terms of the expenses experienced in a certain 12-month period, variously defined in terms of a calendar year, landlord fiscal year, municipal tax year, or lease year. Above the base level as defined, the tenant pays for its pro rata share of property taxes and operating expenses. Tenants are sometimes directly responsible for all cleaning and electricity expenses within their leased area and generally pay their pro rata share of these and other expenses incurred for common areas.

Typically, in a net lease agreement a tenant commits to rent all the space in a building for a specified net rent payable to the landlord. The tenant is responsible for all property taxes and operating expenses; the landlord may or may not have responsibility for exterior and structural repairs for an interim period or for the full lease term. Advantages to the tenant of the net lease concept include the elimination of the multiple profit center problem common in the gross lease and the opportunity to operate and control the building during the period of occupancy.

Landlords will generally attempt to prohibit sublet and assignment rights of leased space to new tenants. Even if they relent, they will try to insert a full or partial right to recapture any incremental rental profit over the level of rent agreed to contractually by the original tenant. If at all possible, landlord profit recapture should be resisted. Sublet or assignment arrangements can be the source of a stream of incremental rental profits, which on a "netting-out" basis can reduce the aggregate corporate rent and occupancy expenses over a number of years. Indeed, in corporate financial reorganization and bankruptcy situations, actualization of a corporation's leasehold advantages as a tenant may spell the difference between corporate survival and extinction.

If properly negotiated, rent renewal, purchase, and right of first refusal options can provide tenants with significant economic benefits. Rent renewal and purchase options in the form of predetermined rental or purchase dollar amounts can confer substantial economic advantages when these options prove to be below open-market levels at the points at which they can be exercised. Such options provide protection for the investments in leasehold improvements which, even if fully amortized at the point of lease expiration for financial accounting purposes, may still have a value-in-use to the corporate tenant. The tenant can often avoid the new capital expenditures which would be incurred for leasehold improvements at an alternative location. Even if a purchase option is not exercised by the tenant, the availability of such an option may enable the tenant to negotiate one or more new renewal periods at an equitable arm's-length market rent or on a more advantageous rental basis. Such options mitigate the landlord's leverage, which is created by the tenant's prior capital investment in leasehold improvements.

When market conditions allow and a tenant has major space usage in a building, the tenant should seek rights of first refusal to lease additional space and to purchase the property. If obtainable, the right of first refusal for additional space may protect the major tenant from the creation of a future dysfunctional use situation. After a major leasehold investment, a tenant may experience a rapid expansion of activity and the need for substantial additional space to house such operations. If the tenant has no leverage for obtaining expansion space in the building, the result can be multiple locations for a relatively integrated process and the consequent impairment of economic and efficient operation. If available, rights of first refusal to lease additional space or to purchase the building should be acquired as part of a strategy to protect the tenant's position. Yet, even if carefully worded, rights of first refusal may either be defeated or be expensive to exercise. It is often difficult for a corporate tenant to verify the actual existence of a legitimate arm's-length, third-party offer; to pinpoint the precise details of the economic structure of the proposed purchase; and to arrive at an accurate assessment of the ability of a potential purchaser to consummate the transaction.

The long-term implications of appropriate leasing practices for corporate control and reduction of rent and occupancy expenses are staggering. Failure to recognize and understand the bottom-line impacts of technical points in lease negotiations can be economically devastating. Those corporations that are professional and businesslike in their approach to space leasing will have a decided advantage over those that are uninformed about technical issues in leasing. A preponderance of leased space has an accelerating effect on rent and occupancy expenses and increases a corporation's exposure to the risks of sustained boom periods, evidenced by a dramatic escalation in market rent levels.

Ownership

There are certain basic investment benefits which can accrue to a business enterprise from the ownership of real estate:

1. Cash flow derived from renting all or a portion of a property to other tenants.

2. Income tax shelter benefits derived from depreciation and mortgage interest deductions for income tax purposes, which shelter a fixed amount of income from federal and state taxes.

3. Receipt of periodic refinancing proceeds without any immediate income tax payments.

4. Possible appreciation in the property's market value which can be actualized at point of future sale.

Ownership of real estate also enables a firm to operate and control a property in a manner most suited to pursuing its own strategic objectives in a direct and efficient fashion. For example, by controlling building operations, a corporation can eliminate profit margins to certain outside service providers and maximize operating expense efficiencies. By enlarging the portion of space inventory which it owns, a firm can often limit the seemingly relentless upward spiral of rent and occupancy expenses. In determining what portion of a firm's space needs are to be met through direct ownership, the firm must calculate the investment yield likely to be received from a specific property as compared to the yield obtainable by investing equivalent capital in its own primary business activities.

There may be some occasions where a decision to own is prudent, even when a higher rate of return could be achieved by a firm's capital investment in its primary business activities. If highly sensitive and essential business functions are conducted in a leased facility, a business firm may be exposed to pressure from a landlord who would seek to take advantage of the tenant's need for continuous and uninterrupted occupancy by demanding a new rent above prevailing market levels at a future point of lease renewal.

Lease-versus-Purchase Analysis

Corporate real estate managers often have to decide whether to lease a particular property or to buy it. The decision may arise when the corporation is first occupying a facility or when a purchase option matures. The decision is a complex one involving qualitative and quantitative factors.

The qualitative factors should be analyzed against the background of the corporate real estate plan. Questions to be asked include these:

1. How willing is the corporation to manage its own facility?

2. How difficult will it be to deal with the prospective landlord if the decision is made to lease?

3. How much control does this particular sector of the corporation require over its premises?

The quantitative factors can be analyzed on the basis of a simple comparison of the benefits and costs of the purchase and lease scenarios. In order to perform the analysis the following data should be assembled:

1. Terms of the prospective lease, including
   a. Base rentals with mandated future changes
   b. Operating costs (unless the contemplated lease will be a net lease)
   c. Term
   d. Fixed-rent renewal options, if any
2. Terms of the prospective purchase, including
   a. Total purchase price
   b. Percentage of price financed by the corporation and percentage financed by outside sources
   c. Cost of capital for internal financing and debt service for external financing
   d. Estimated operating expenses, if purchase is being compared to a gross lease

With the above data, a cash flow can be generated for each of the lease and purchase scenarios for a specified time frame. If the analysis includes all inflows and outflows, then it would seem logical that the cash flow with the lowest present value cost would be most favorable to the corporation.

However, one further factor must be examined. If the firm elects to purchase, the facility will have a residual present value at the end of the term selected for analysis. If the difference between the lease and purchase cash flows (present value of cost of purchase cash flow minus present value of cost of lease cash flow) is less than the manager's educated guess as to the value of the facility at the end of the term (discounted back to present value), the obvious decision would be to purchase; otherwise, the manager should elect to lease.

A numerical analysis is useful in a situation where all other factors are equal. It should be utilized only after the qualitative factors have been analyzed and the acquisition has been determined to fit the guidelines of the long-range real estate plan.

Sale-Leaseback

The sale-leaseback, as its name implies, involves relinquishing long-term control of an asset (land, building, air rights) in return for receipt of an up-front payment and the right to lease the same asset. Often associated with major properties, the sale-leaseback can be effected using air rights, equipment, and a variety of other assets.

Until recently, sale-leasebacks have been useful off-balance-sheet financing tools for corporations requiring cash. For the corporation with triple-

A credit, the resulting lease payments may make the effective financing cost even more attractive, especially if the opportunity cost of capital invested in owned facilities is taken into account. Although changes in the tax laws have slowed such use of the sale-leaseback, it may still be useful for the corporation which owns its facilities but does not require long-term control—for example, scattered retail uses.

Exchanging an owned facility for a leased one generally results in increased rent and occupancy expenses for the corporation which intends to occupy its facilities for the long term. Although as a debt instrument the sale-leaseback may be financially attractive, the eventual cost of occupying the facility must be carefully studied. Many corporations have good reasons to lease and prefer to do so, but analysis of comparable rent and occupancy expenses from income statements in a particular industry will almost always reveal that rent and occupancy expenses are historically lower in corporations which own a large proportion of their real estate portfolio. This often may be true even after an adjustment in ratios for the opportunity cost issue. A careful analysis of the long-term effects of selling and leasing back should be performed before such a transaction is approved.

Joint Venture

A real estate development joint venture is the combination of two or more partners for the purpose of developing one or a series of properties. In corporate real estate the classic form has been the alliance of a corporation that will be the anchor tenant with an entrepreneurial real estate developer who possesses the necessary experience and expertise to develop the proposed project.

The corporation's usual contribution may be its commitment to lease space and, possibly, to contribute the site. The developer's contributions may include the planning, financing, construction, marketing, and management of the development. There may be a tug-of-war about who contributes cash and carries deficits. From a corporate real estate perspective the goal is to make these burdens the responsibility of the real estate developer. The corporation also would like completion and capital cost guarantees.

The corporation's equity interest may be specifically identified in the property deed, which denotes the traditional concept of ownership. An alternative is for the corporation to have a carried interest in the property, which entitles it by agreement with the joint-venture partner to a percentage share of cash flow, tax shelter, refinancing benefits, and resale proceeds. For balance-sheet or other financial or regulatory purposes, some corporations may prefer a carried interest in lieu of the traditional form of ownership identified in a deed.

The corporation, by choosing a specific development site, possibly making a land contribution, and committing to lease a portion of the space, often gives a newly proposed development the visible momentum and creditworthiness necessary to obtain financing and additional tenants. The corporate partner should seek to lease the space it will occupy at a competitive rental rate. There should be preference returns on actual cash and land investments; first returns to the corporation, then to the developer, and then the residual profits to be allocated on a predetermined basis.

The advantage of the joint-venture mode to the corporation is the acquisition of a seasoned real estate development partner who has the ability to conceive, plan, finance, build, market, and manage the real estate development and who takes much of the exposure to risk. The developer's advantages are the corporation's benefit-conferring choice of the specified development and the commitment to lease space and the possible contribution of a site.

The disadvantages of such joint-venture arrangements may include disputes during the planning, developmental, or holding phases or a default by one of the partners. Another problem is that each partner holds a fractional percentage of ownership in the real estate development, and liquidating one partner's position in order to actualize property appreciation benefits may prove cumbersome. A good precaution is a predetermined method for a possible future separation and divestiture of the respective interests. This result may be accomplished by means of a buy-sell mechanism, an arbitration proceeding, or a right of first refusal by each partner on any sale to a third party. As previously noted, a right of first refusal may be difficult in its application.

Leasing as a Joint-Venture Variant

Leasing arrangements may be employed as variants on the joint-venture arrangement. Under the master lease concept a corporation may commit to lease an entire to-be-built facility and then grant an operating lease to the developer for the portion of the space it does not actually intend to occupy. The developer, in turn, leases space to third parties. The master lease concept lends the anchor tenant's credit strength to the development, facilitating project financing. The corporation, in turn, generally obtains the developer's guarantee that the additional unrequired space will be sublet and that the developer will carry any deficit until all such tenants are in occupancy and paying rent. In exchange for entering into the master lease, the anchor tenant receives an ownership or carried interest in the property. The risk to the corporate tenant is that it is ultimately responsible for rent payments on the entire property if the developer does not lease the remaining space to other tenants in a timely fashion and is unable to support the carrying costs.

Another form of leasing as a joint-venture variant involves a corporation which may need a portion of the space in a proposed facility but makes a lease commitment to take a larger amount of space. This major lease commitment builds market acceptance and momentum for the project and aids in the attainment of suitable financing. The corporate tenant's risk is the need to sublet the excess space in a timely fashion if it is to avoid paying rent for space it does not require for its own operations. In exchange for these contributions to the future success of the project, the corporation receives an ownership or carried interest in the property and the consequent benefits which enable the corporation to reduce its rent and occupancy expenses. Both of these leasing devices are employed to find a creative solution to profit generation and the reduction of rent and occupancy expenses, but neither method is without risk.

A third joint-venture leasing variant involves the landlord's granting the tenant a partial ownership or carried interest position as an added inducement for leasing a portion of the space in the property in question. Generally, this type of arrangement is most easily achieved in a soft rental market or because the tenant's rent has been increased above the going rate in order to compensate the landlord for giving up a portion of the benefits associated with the equity position. Such an arrangement may also occur when a landlord has no actual cash investment in the property, having financed out, and wishes to shorten the absorption period in order to avoid exposure to a negative carry burden. In such situations, tenants should solicit rental offerings which alternatively do and do not convey an equity interest. In this way, the tenant may quantify analytically the cost of obtaining equity. When a landlord proposes to convey fractional equity positions to tenants with unilateral buy-back provisions priced by a predetermined mathematical formula, the tenant may have been given a relatively cosmetic equity without the full benefits of ownership.

Corporation as Sole Developer

When a corporation acts independently as the developer of real estate, it eliminates the disadvantages inherent in the structure of any joint-venture arrangement, completely owns the property, and controls its own destiny.

For many corporations, acting as sole developer has its own built-in disadvantages. Most corporations do not have in-house real estate development experience and expertise. The corporation's compensation practices and decision-making processes may make it difficult to attract real estate entrepreneurs for in-house real estate development positions. Even if the difficulties in finding the appropriate experts can be overcome, the difficulties inherent in the development process should never be underestimated. If the senior management of a corporation can come to understand

and adjust to the major differences between the corporation's usual business activities and the complexities and volatile nature of development activities, a significant new source of corporate profits may be possible.

Syndication

A syndication involves the combination of an experienced real estate professional as general partner with a group of passive investors—generally without substantial real estate experience—as the limited partners. A syndication is formed to develop or acquire real estate. The general partner or his employees and agents perform the necessary property management, leasing, marketing, and sales activities associated with accomplishing profit objectives.

In a corporate real estate context, a syndication vehicle may be utilized to sell certain benefits of property ownership such as tax shelter, which may be more valuable to the syndicate's partners than to a major corporation with sufficient tax shelter from other sources.

Syndicators sometimes buy real estate from corporations at prices in excess of those obtainable from more traditional real estate investors. In turn, the syndication's general partner benefits from the fees generated by the syndication and ongoing management of the asset and from the residual benefits of any retained ownership or refinancing benefits.

The limited partners' advantages are the opportunity to obtain the traditional benefits of real estate ownership with liability generally limited to the amount of the cash investment and any specific commitment for additional calls on capital and certain income tax recapture problems, if there should be a foreclosure. The burden of managing the real estate asset remains with the syndicator-general partner.

If a corporation sells a real estate asset to a syndicator and takes back a purchase money mortgage for a portion of the sales price, it may later experience a mortgage default if the syndication has been improperly structured or if asset management goals and activities are unrealistic or have been improperly executed. Corporate real estate units should deal cautiously in this area.

Project Funding

A corporation's source of funds for capital investments in real estate are many and varied. Some business enterprises are so profitable and have such substantial cash flows from their primary activities that capital requirements for corporate real estate projects are totally funded from internally generated cash flow. For example, certain heavily capitalized and highly profitable consumer product companies often have used such a funding source.

Another financing device is the sale of various forms of corporate indebtedness, which, depending on the financial strength of a specific corporation, are sold with or without the guarantee of a financial institution. A revolving-credit term loan facility granted to a business corporation by a commercial bank or insurance company is another external source of funds. There is an initial funding period as a project is constructed and then a point at which there is a conversion to a term loan, which may feature full or partial amortization over the remaining years of the loan. Loan agreements generally define the purpose to which the proceeds may be applied and are further structured with affirmative and negative convenants and specified events for default, which, in effect, provide the boundaries within which a firm must operate its business. These loan conditions are agreed to by the corporate borrower as a comfort to the creditor and as issues which must be satisfied as conditions precedent to a lender's extension of credit. Project-focused revolving loans are common in heavy industrial process construction projects.

Utilization of a construction loan is sometimes the chosen means of raising funds for a specific project. The prospective construction lender, generally a commercial bank, will pursue the investigation and analysis of the facts and assumptions relating to the borrower's track record of accomplishments, current financial condition, and long-term business prospects, the local real estate market conditions, the economic feasibility and likely market value upon project completion, and the construction and legal issues. After the construction loan is approved, funds are advanced periodically on the basis of the percentage of work in place or on a staged basis, less a retainage amount. In the final financing phase a permanent (intermediate or long-term) lender, such as an insurance company or a thrift institution, is often the mortgage holder.

Property or Air Rights Sales

In some mature corporations, many properties were acquired or leased in much earlier periods of corporate history. Often such properties were built in compliance with prior zoning regulations and subject to different market conditions. The result is that corporate portfolios today contain some properties where air rights and the improvements themselves are worth more as real estate assets than as going businesses. One way to tap some of the value is to sell the air rights (the right to build additional square footage).

Since many corporations will not allow the sale of an essential facility to extract its real estate value, the sale of air rights allows the building to remain in corporate ownership and use while still realizing some value from the unused air rights. The value of the air rights may be limited because of the restricted number of potential buyers (in many jurisdictions adjacent property owners only) and because any construction activity would have to accommodate the corporation's ongoing business at the site. However, value can sometimes be increased because the property may be treated as a holdout, or it may be the key parcel necessary for such zoning bonuses as plazas and arcades, which, when provided, generally allow a developer to build a taller building as a quid pro quo. Through such air right sales, it is possible both to satisfy the corporation's business requirements and to extract significant value from the real estate.

Certain real estate assets in a corporation's portfolio become surplus. Such properties are no longer logistically relevant for the fulfillment of a firm's primary business objectives. In order to maximize the proceeds to be received from the sale of such properties, it is important to identify the highest and best reuse of the property and then to design and execute a marketing program which capitalizes on such conclusions. For example, highway patterns have changed, the ideal configuration of gasoline stations has evolved, and the inventory of gasoline stations has outstripped the ability of the marketplace to support them all economically. Many gasoline stations have proved to be redundant. Some of them have been sold for minimal prices. In other cases the identification of imaginative new uses, such as liquor stores, dry cleaning establishments, and convenience food stores, have made possible the achievement of greater economic benefits.

Unconsolidated Real Estate Subsidiary

The unconsolidated subsidiary concept is popular in certain industries. This concept can be used as a financing device for one or more real estate transactions, and it may also be the organizational focal point for certain corporate real estate activities, generally, those which are more entrepreneurial in nature.

Depending on the accounting, financial, legal, income tax, and regulatory circumstances of specific corporations and industries, the unconsolidated subsidiary structure may provide the opportunity for property collateralized by mortgage debt with no recourse to the parent corporation to be removed from the financial statement of the parent. The unconsolidated subsidiary may enable a higher leveraging of the debt-to-value relationship of individual properties without any direct effect on the parent corporation's debt-to-equity ratio. At the same time, the income tax benefits of real estate ownership can still benefit the parent corporation since, for this purpose, an unconsolidated subsidiary's real estate activities are consolidated with the financial results of the parent. Many real estate transactions, particularly those not associated with the parent corporation's occupancy of space, may be conducted in the unconsolidated subsidiary form.

According to generally accepted accounting principles, in order to protect the subsidiary's unconsolidated status, its activities must be basically nonessential to the core activities of the parent corporation, so that the extinction of the subsidiary would not threaten the survival of the parent. In addition, the unconsolidated subsidiary must be engaged primarily in activities with third parties. The parent must not be an ongoing source of funding and the unconsolidated subsidiary's debt must be without recourse to the parent firm.

This concept may be utilized as a financing vehicle or a real estate brokerage operation. The entity may also buy, sell, lease, or develop property. If such a subsidiary is effective, it may reduce rent and occupancy expenses for the parent as well as develop new sources of corporate profits. Before setting up an unconsolidated subsidiary, the concept should be reviewed with the chief financial officer and legal counsel.*

Conclusion

The implications of the strategies made, and the degree of success of the management and real estate techniques employed, to implement the selected strategic objectives can have a dramatic positive or negative impact on the corporation's bottom line. Strategies for corporate real estate have broad implications for the firm's future market share, expansion potential, and overall profitability.

---

* Readers who have a greater interest in this subject should consult *The Unconsolidated Real Estate Subsidiary: A Technique to Finance Corporate Real Estate* by David M. Bick, published in booklet form by Salomon Brothers' Corporate Real Estate Group.

5

Organizing, Staffing, and Compensating the Corporate Real Estate Function

Sandford I. Gadient

President, Huntress Real Estate Executive Search, Inc.

Ralph C. Hook, Jr.

Professor of Marketing, University of Hawaii; Senior Consultant/Director Research Department, Huntress Real Estate Executive Search, Inc.

Corporate real estate is almost always viewed as a means to an end, namely, providing facilities to accomplish the corporation's mainstream operation. There is no single proper organizational structure to fit all companies. A structure must be custom-designed to suit the unique circumstances of each corporation's needs. After the proper organizational structure has been determined, the actual staffing of the real estate function with capable executives is every bit as important as, if not more important than, the organizational structure itself. Finally, in order to attract, motivate, and retain the executives performing both the generalist and the specialist functions within the real estate activity, it is vital to design a realistic compensation program based on real estate industry benchmarks as well as internal corporate measures. This essay will address each of these subjects and is divided accordingly.

Organizing the Corporate Real Estate Function

In conducting numerous real estate organizational studies throughout the nation over the last 15 years, Huntress Real Estate Executive Search, Inc., discovered that while each corporation has unique real estate requirements, answers to the following questions must usually be sought before the proper organizational structure can be designed:

1. What stage of growth is the corporation experiencing and how does it impact on its real estate activities?

2. What specialized functions need to be performed by the corporation's real estate activity?

3. Should a separate real estate subsidiary be organized to handle some or all of the corporation's real estate activities?

4. How does the corporation's present organizational structure operate, relative both to centralized versus decentralized decision making and to geographical requirements?

5. Where should the real estate function be positioned within the overall corporate organizational framework?

6. Has a comprehensive real estate operations and procedures manual been prepared to allow real estate responsibilities for investment, operations, and profit to be matched with appropriate levels of authority, responsibility, and accountability?

Corporate Growth Stage

The example given in Table 5.1 relates to a major industrial company. Retail companies, service companies, and other types of firms also experience expansion cycles that, while different in their particulars from industrial corporations, still generally require a specialized real estate activity responsive to each particular growth stage.

Specialized Real Estate Functions

What specialized functions need to be performed by a corporation's real estate unit? Again, while each corporation is unique, in conducting organizational studies, we have found a need for the types of skills enumerated in Figure 5.1, which depicts a typical organizational structure of a corporate real estate activity, including major related functions. It should be noted that while each function is shown as a separate box, this does not mean each function (or subfunction) should necessarily be staffed by a full-time executive. Instead, the volume level of activity, complexity of the transactions, and level of risk and reward should be measured before determining the actual staff necessary to direct each specialized function.

Separate Real Estate Subsidiary

Corporations sometimes initially organize their real estate activity as a department within the finance or law units. This happens because real estate is closely related to, and seriously impacts, both finance and law. As corporations expand, the real estate function is frequently organized, in part or entirely, as a separate subsidiary for some or all of the following reasons:

1. If it is a separate corporate entity, the performance of real estate can be measured more easily.

2. Sometimes related real estate debt can be accumulated as an off-balance sheet item in the overall financial statements, thereby improving certain overall corporate financial ratios, e.g., debt to equity.

3. A subsidiary's board of directors can maintain overall control by inclusion of key financial executives, e.g., financial vice president, controller, or treasurer, and still react more rapidly than the parent corporate board, which may meet less frequently and have a longer agenda.

4. With real estate being separated into a subsidiary, it is more practical to charge operating entities true market rates for occupancy, thereby fairly measuring various operating units without distortions due to windfalls from historic conditions.

5. By separating each major real estate venture into a separate corporation, some companies feel that, should a financial disaster strike a particular project and eliminate the subsidiary's equity, the parent and other related entities can negotiate a better settlement than if each transaction is the parent company's full financial responsibility.

While no hard-and-fast rules exist as to which organizational format is best, in general the separate subsidiary is more conducive to a for-profit approach to doing business in a less political atmosphere and, thus, while currently unusual (perhaps 20 to 25 percent of major corporations today use the subsidiary format), this form of organization allows the corpora-

Table 5.1. Growth Stages of the Corporate Real Estate Function

Product company life cycle	Real estate requirements	Real estate organization structure	Number of real estate locations	Real estate staff
Invention and initial pilot production/marketing	Frequently housed in homes, garages, or low-rent, readily available quarters	What little attention directed to real estate is usually handled by founder	1	None
Preliminary mass production/marketing of product/service	Small facility to handle production, distribution, and office functions of company	Real estate usually consists of leased quarters with decision generally still being made by founder or founder's top financial circle	2 to 6	One, part-time
Rapid expansion of product/service requires local (perhaps within several states) geographic decentralization to service market demands	Multiple facilities to handle manufacturing, distribution, and office functions spread over area of several states	Usually a main office (frequently company-owned) will be built at this stage, utilizing outside talent, which then requires limited-facility management; also, leasing or construction expertise may be required for regional growth	7 to 12	One, full-time, plus secretary and perhaps an assistant

Expansion into major regional presence	Facilities owned are being expanded while new locations are being leased or constructed throughout entire region; frequently the administrative headquarters will be separated from production/marketing facilities, thereby causing an expansion of real estate activity	Leasing, management, construction, legal, and finance real estate expertise will be required for the regional real estate operation	13 to 50	Several executives plus several administrators
Further expansion into national company with the start of overseas operations	Administrative headquarters may be divided into several groupings, and economies of scale usually dictate expansion/consolidation of selected facilities and closing/disposition of earlier, smaller locations	Usually headed by a vice president-real estate (or senior vice president). The activity would include all functions of real estate and may also involve for-profit development in the United States	51 to 500	Vice president-real estate plus three or more real estate directors
Multinational offices and facilities doing business throughout the world	Administrative, production, marketing, and warehousing facilities need to be properly housed, not just in the United States but also in all major countries, in some cases in wholly/partially owned subsidiaries	All functional areas of real estate know-how must be represented, and often company's owned real estate allows for development opportunities for profit without regard to company's own use	Over 500	Perhaps executive vice president or president plus vice president's in functional positions and related staffs

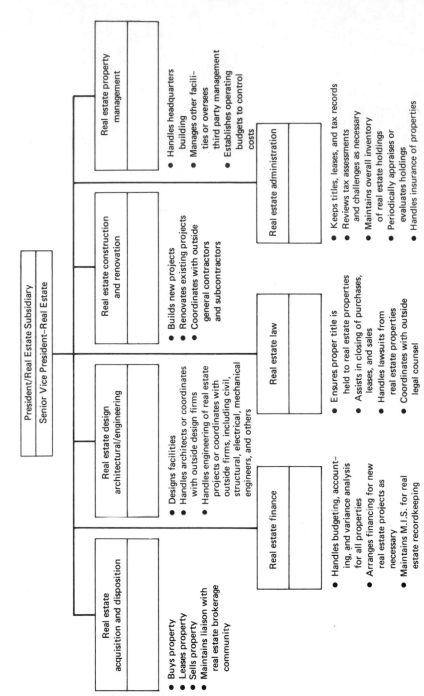

Figure 5.1. Organizational structure of corporate real estate activity including major related functions.

Real estate acquisition and disposition
- Buys property
- Leases property
- Sells property
- Maintains liaison with real estate brokerage community

Real estate design architectural/engineering
- Designs facilities
- Handles architects or coordinates with outside design firms
- Handles engineering of real estate projects or coordinates with outside firms, including civil, structural, electrical, mechanical engineers, and others

Real estate construction and renovation
- Builds new projects
- Renovates existing projects
- Coordinates with outside general contractors and subcontractors

Real estate property management
- Handles headquarters building
- Manages other facilities or oversees third party management
- Establishes operating budgets to control costs

President/Real Estate Subsidiary

Senior Vice President–Real Estate

Real estate finance
- Handles budgeting, accounting, and variance analysis for all properties
- Arranges financing for new real estate projects as necessary
- Maintains M.I.S. for real estate recordkeeping

Real estate law
- Ensures proper title is held to real estate properties
- Assists in closing of purchases, leases, and sales
- Handles lawsuits from real estate properties
- Coordinates with outside legal counsel

Real estate administration
- Keeps titles, leases, and tax records
- Reviews tax assessments and challenges as necessary
- Maintains overall inventory of real estate holdings
- Periodically appraises or evaluates holdings
- Handles insurance of properties

tions that use it to attract more capable real estate executives and compensate them realistically.

Centralized versus Decentralized Decision Making

Historically, industrial corporations in this country began as highly centralized organizations with tight controls on decision making. As multiple-product companies became the vogue and the successes of decentralized companies like General Motors and General Electric became legend, many organizations sought to decentralize their activities to the lowest level of logical profit-center responsibility. In some respects, highly centralized management is again becoming popular as attempts are made to compete with lost-cost competitors from overseas.

Relating real estate decisions to the entire organizational fabric of U.S. corporations, it appears that decentralized decision making never reached the real estate function to the same extent that it did other activities. In real estate, however, local knowledge of market conditions, market prices, and market opportunities is critical to success. Thus, the ideal framework is often one which is highly centralized from a planning standpoint but somewhat decentralized from the standpoint of execution. For example, if a company has five or six different divisions that need office space in a major metropolitan area, several may be growing quite rapidly, others may be constant, and some may actually have declining needs for space. Real estate decisions can be made from the standpoint of meeting present needs or anticipating future needs. Regardless of which method is used, by consolidating all five divisions' requirements for office space into a single facility—whether owned or leased—a significant saving should be realized, as opposed to contracting separately to meet each need. To the extent that business is being conducted nationally or internationally, thereby requiring extensive facilities, it is always necessary to have comprehensive knowledge of local conditions, which can be gained by involving local management, including regional real estate specialists, or hiring knowledgeable local consultants.

Positioning Real Estate in the Overall Corporate Organizational Structure

To determine where real estate fits within any particular corporation's organizational structure, two questions must be answered. One, can a structure be devised that is sufficiently compact to allow real estate opportunities to be evaluated and acted upon in a timely fashion? Two, despite the continued need for fast decisions (after all, an opportunity missed is profit foregone), are sufficient controls programmed into the process to assure that corporate assets are protected? In general, as real estate becomes more important to the success of an enterprise, the top real estate executives' status within the organization rises. Figure 5.2 indicates three different approaches to positioning the real estate operation in different types of companies, all of which can respond to these two questions.

Real Estate Operations Manual

In order to properly organize a corporate real estate function, it is necessary to have a simple and straightforward operations manual which covers the procedures necessary to buy, sell, lease, and sublease as well as to construct and manage property. Each procedure should carefully spell out the "who, what, where, why, how, and when" aspects of the subject, as well as establish limits of commitment appropriate to various levels of authority. Such a manual should be used as a guide to conducting transactions by the real estate group as well as any real estate matters handled by operating departments. To indicate the detail needed, the table of contents of a real estate department operations manual for a corporation doing business primarily through franchises is outlined in Figure 5.3.

Checklist of Frequent Mistakes in Organizing Corporate Real Estate Activities

When organizing or reorganizing a real estate unit, it is vital to avoid the following major pitfalls:

1. Lack of a well-defined operating plan that includes detailed operating and capital budgets for the real estate activity

2. Lack of a readily available, comprehensive list of all properties, both operating and excess

3. Failure to maintain a constantly up-to-date comprehensive list of all uses

4. Failure to target excess properties for disposition—to recycle monies into the company—with the same care that expansion properties are purchased

5. Insufficient responsiveness of the real estate activity to the needs of operating business centers within the company, resulting in disruption and inefficiency

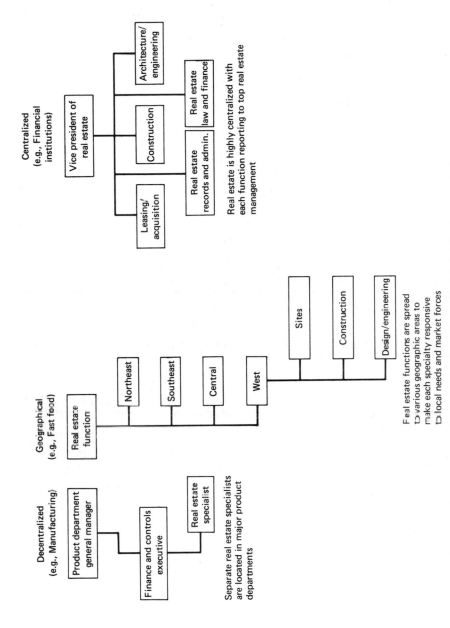

Figure 5.2. Alternative organizational structures for positioning real estate function in corporate decision making.

Table of Contents

Chapter 1	Organization
Chapter 2	Objectives, functions, and activities
Chapter 3	Job descriptions
Chapter 4	Purchase document
Chapter 5	Ground lease document
Chapter 6	Site layouts
Chapter 7	Site criteria
Chapter 8	Site submittal package
Chapter 9	Site appraisals
Chapter 10	Approval process
Chapter 11	Market development plan
Chapter 12	Conflict of interest
Chapter 13	Travel advances
Chapter 14	Standard signage
Chapter 15	Miscellaneous forms
Chapter 16	Franchise relationship
Chapter 17	Approval process-special projects
Chapter 18	Sales projections
Chapter 19	Broker involvement
Chapter 20	Franchise development, program policy

Figure 5.3. Real estate department operations manual—table of contents.

6. Failure to create a competitive compensation program for corporate real estate executives
7. Failure of evaluation program to measure key executives' accomplishments against well-defined quantitative and qualitative goals to determine increases in the base salary and payment of incentive bonuses

Staffing the Corporate Real Estate Function

Competent Corporate Real Estate Experts

Where can competent corporate real estate executives be found? There are a number of sources. Among them are

1. Your own real estate department
2. Other company departments, such as legal and finance
3. Other corporate real estate departments
4. The real estate brokerage community

5. The real estate property and asset management community
6. The real estate development and construction community

The Nuances of Corporate Real Estate

Is real estate sufficiently complicated to require specialized knowledge or can generally competent corporate managers quickly learn the nuances of corporate real estate? Specialists in finance, engineering, research and development, manufacturing, and marketing have long training programs and considerable depth of knowledge. Real estate activity is becoming equally specialized, and if 20 to 25 percent of a company's assets are committed to real estate, broadly experienced real estate generalists and deeply skilled real estate specialists should be combined into a smoothly functioning real estate activity.

Interviewing the Corporate Real Estate Executive

Thousands of real estate executives are interviewed each year, both by telephone and in person. The following checklist of major job applicant vital signs can assist employers in getting the most out of each interview. Knowledgeable employers realize that there are basic points to review which give a fundamental picture of the candidate. It is unlikely that a person will attain high marks for each and every vital sign, but an overall high rating will maximize the chances of success on the job. It is also important to keep in mind that different types of positions require different talents, skills, intelligence, experience, and levels of education.

Interviewing potential real estate executives is an imperfect process at best. Experience, coupled with careful review of these vital signs, will help take some of the guesswork out of employee selection. Also, having the candidate interviewed by several knowledgeable executives in the company often yields a more balanced perspective than merely relying on the opinion of one executive who makes the hiring decision.

INTERVIEW CHECKLIST

1. ATTITUDE: Does the person have a positive attitude? Evidence of this will often be a cheerful and helpful nature and a friendly smile.

2. OBJECTIVE: Does the person have a career objective? How does it match with those of the position for which he or she is being recruited?

3. APPEARANCE: Does this person show pride in clothing and grooming? If so, then performance will probably reflect this same pride and attention.

4. EXPERIENCE: Does this person have sufficient exposure to technical competence at the level expected of the position? What is the individual's past job performance record? What are the principal accomplishments to date?

5. STABILITY: How many different jobs has the person held? What was the length of time on each job? What was the reason for leaving each job?

6. EDUCATION: How much formal education has this person had? What specialized areas? Class standing? Extracurricular activities? Honors and awards? Schools attended?

7. LEARNING: What are this person's continuing learning and areas of specialization? Professional designations? Participation in professional and career-oriented organizations? Offices held? Career changes?

8. REFERENCES: What do others say about this person? Former employers, coworkers, employees, and business and personal acquaintances are excellent sources. How does the candidate relate to these people?

9. ENERGY: Is the person physically healthy and active? Has the get-up-and-go gotten up and gone? Can the candidate stand the pressures of the job with mental and physical strength to spare? Does he or she like to get out in the field or prefer to stay in an ivory tower?

10. INTEGRITY: Does the person understand and practice fair business ethics? Can his or her word be relied upon? Do people trust this person? Does he or she transmit confidence by word and deed?

11. MATURITY: Is the person wise beyond his or her years? Does this individual have good manners and avoid childish statements and actions? Can he or she rise above a difficult situation?

12. MOTIVATION: Is the person a self-starter? Is he or she a leader or a follower? Will this person go the extra mile and then some? Can he or she provide the environment so that other people will be motivated to take positive action?

13. INTELLIGENCE: Is the person capable of learning and understanding? Can he or she make decisions quickly, fairly, and correctly? Does the person possess the resources to fulfill the requirements of the position and also to advance further? Can he or she keep things simple?

14. MANAGERIAL: Does this person make the best use of time and talent? Avoid unnecessary waste? Direct others in an efficient manner?

15. PERSONALITY: Do others respect as well as like the individual? Does he or she make others feel that they also have something to contribute?

Does the person know how to work alone and as a team player? Is he or she so busy with self-improvement that there is no time to criticize others?

16. SERVICE: Does the person contribute to the community as well as the profession? Is the individual aware that great personal satisfaction can be realized through sharing?

Importance of Organization Charts and Operating Relationships

Organization charts provide only a static picture of the corporate structure and, therefore, have limitations. Where properly prepared, however, the organizational chart indicates the reporting relationships as well as staff relationships. This is especially important for the real estate function, which is frequently not charted. Because organization charts are in such widespread use, no example is included. The key point is that line and staff relationships of the real estate function must be properly charted.

Detailed Position Descriptions— Areas of Major Emphasis

Position descriptions should indicate to whom the person reports, basic functions of the position, major responsibilities, and qualifications for the job. A sample of a position description is illustrated in Figure 5.4 to indicate the detail that is needed.

Entry-Level Training Programs That Get Results

No modern, rapidly expanding, well-managed company can do without several training programs to infuse new talent into the mainstream of the company's activities. Typical training programs include the marketing, research and development, product, and finance functions. Yet, almost without exception, specialized training programs do not exist in corporate America to develop capable and well-rounded real estate executives.

Such a program, to be successful, must do the following things:

1. Attract several bright and well-trained college and business school graduates each year

2. Offer a broad program of on-the-job exposure to all major real estate functions, with frequent performance reviews

3. Integrate special courses, taught by company or industry professionals, into the training program

REPORTS TO: Senior Vice President, Real Estate Division

BASIC FUNCTIONS: The Vice President-Office Building Development is responsible for all phases of development leading to completed and occupied office buildings. The incumbent reports to and is responsible for assisting the Senior Vice President-Real Estate in evaluating office building acquisitions and/or development of office buildings.

MAJOR RESPONSIBILITIES:
1. Evaluates and selects office building acquisition opportunities.
2. Evaluates and selects sites for development into office buildings.
3. Coordinates and directs market research and demographic studies to determine the feasibility of sites for future development and/or acquisition.
4. Develops relationships with the financial community and other business concerns whose assistance is helpful in identifying office space needs.
5. With facilities planning and legal counsel, reviews zoning, municipal, and regional requirements and determines what changes would be required to permit development or expansion opportunities in the event of acquisition.
6. With the assistance of facilities planning, determines environmental impediments that would make the property prohibitive or legally impossible to develop.
7. Provides finance division with sufficient data to prepare appropriate analysis and definitive estimates of potential developments.
8. Negotiates options to purchase property for development and/or building acquisition and also negotiates leases with tenants.
9. As a key manager, provides input for the company's planning process.
10. Participates in establishing property management program for completed office buildings.
11. Assists in developing project marketing and leasing plan strategies.
12. Works with facilities planning to establish financially sound and marketable office building design.
13. Prepares reports and provides information for use in securing long-term project financing.
14. With facilities planning, represents the project in all relationships with municipality, government agencies, community organizations, and other agencies.

QUALIFICATIONS:
This person should possess
1. A thorough understanding of pro forma budgets, office building feasibility studies, and market research.
2. A degree in business or closely related curriculum.
3. Five years' experience in all phases of office building development and acquisitions.
4. A good understanding of marketing and demographic studies.
5. The ability to represent the corporation effectively in all external dealings.
6. A business orientation toward planning and growth.

Figure 5.4. Position description.

4. Assign each trainee to one senior real estate executive to monitor the trainee's overall progress and serve as adviser

5. Insert real estate management trainees into real-life situations to advance their problem-solving abilities and critique the results carefully

6. Ensure that upwardly mobile career paths are available to real estate specialists in various functions (e.g., real estate law, real estate accounting, construction, and site acquisition) as well as real estate generalists who direct one or more of these functions in various departments

7. Ensure that one person in the real estate activity has ongoing responsibility for the success of the training program and expect such a program to consume considerable time of that executive

Importance of Professional Real Estate Societies, Specialized Real Estate Training Courses, and Real Estate Professional Designations

Real estate societies have designed specialized training programs to deal with important and timely topics. NACORE, for example, offers specialized courses in the following areas: negotiations in real estate transactions, industrial location and planning, office space leasing, real estate appraisal and evaluation, retail site selection, and corporate real estate finance. They provide valuable courses at major universities around the nation and certify graduates with the Associate of Corporate Real Estate (ACR) and Master of Corporate Real Estate (MCR) designations, the highest professional certification in the industry. Enrollment in these courses should be made available to management trainees as desired, as well as to more-seasoned executives already working within the real estate function.

Compensating Corporate Real Estate Executives

Are Corporations Fully Compensating Real Estate Executives?

Certain types of companies, such as brokerage firms, developers, and syndicators, are compensating many of their top executives fairly, if not fully. Most industrial, commercial, and financial organizations do not compensate their outstanding real estate executives either fully or fairly. While corporations have over $1 trillion invested in real estate—constituting as

much as 25 percent of many major companies' assets—there is still a belief
that "we are not in the real estate business, we are a widget-maker." This
may result in good real estate executives leaving and being replaced by
castoffs from various administrative functions, a maintenance approach as
opposed to a profit orientation among the staff, many overcharges in purchasing and leasing real estate or lost opportunities in terms of timely dispositions, and top management ignoring the problems of real estate in the
hope they will disappear.

Compensation as Related to Size of Capital Budget, Size of Operating Budget, and Complexity of Real Estate Tasks

Usually the levels of real estate compensation, both for individuals and for
the entire real estate department, relate to the following:

1. *Size of capital budget.* If the company is spending $100 million
annually for real estate and construction, a greater level of expertise and
management depth is required than for a smaller company spending, say,
$10 million.

2. *Size of operating budget.* The larger the real estate department's
operating budget, the higher the level of real estate expertise and compensation required.

3. *Complexity of real estate tasks.* If the corporation is a fast-food
chain building 400 new units a year, each structure quite similar, even
though $100 million may be expended (if the units cost $250,000 each),
the compensation may not be as great as that paid by a specialty restaurant
adding 50 units per year with each unit unique and budgeted at an average
cost of $2 million.

Base Compensation Ranges

Table 5.2 indicates that a typical real estate vice president's compensation
increased 8.6 percent in 1985 to reach $75,500 for base salary and bonus.
Using the upper one-third, the midpoint was $94,800 total cash compen-
sation. At the lower one-third, the midpoint equaled $64,100. Lesser posi-
tions, of course, enjoyed lower levels of compensation.

Bonus Compensation Plans

Most progressive companies today offer incentive programs to stretch the
performance of top real estate professionals. Figure 5.5 demonstrates, for

Table 5.2. Compensation for Selected Positions in Corporate Real Estate

Category position	Lowest/highest compensation		Lowest 1/3 midpoint	Middle 1/3 midpoint	Highest 1/3 midpoint	1985 vs. 1984 % change one year
Vice president—real estate	45,000	140,000	63,200	74,400	93,400	7.1
Properties/operations manager	43,000	86,000	51,600	63,000	79,500	6.3
Attorney	29,000	79,000	36,700	45,200	56,500	5.0
Facilities property administrator	25,000	59,000	34,400	42,500	52,100	6.2
Facilities engineer	26,000	66,000	30,800	43,800	56,200	6.0
Facilities lease negotiator	24,000	68,000	30,500	45,200	56,100	6.6
Asset disvestment manager	45,000	110,000	62,600	73,600	87,200	6.9

SOURCE: Huntress Real Estate Executive Search, Inc., "Annual Compensation Report."

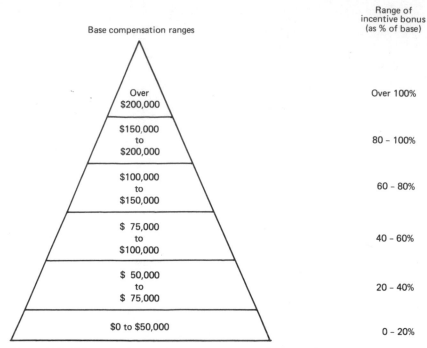

Base compensation ranges

Range of
incentive bonus
(as % of base)

Base compensation ranges	Range of incentive bonus (as % of base)
Over $200,000	Over 100%
$150,000 to $200,000	80 – 100%
$100,000 to $150,000	60 – 80%
$ 75,000 to $100,000	40 – 60%
$ 50,000 to $ 75,000	20 – 40%
$0 to $50,000	0 – 20%

Figure 5.5. Relationship between base compensation and incentive bonus.

various base compensation ranges, the potential range of incentives. For example, in the $50,000 to $100,000 base compensation category, a typical effective incentive program should range from 25 to 50 percent of the base.

Need for Remaining Competitive by the Use of Periodic Compensation Surveys

We suggest that the compensation of corporate real estate executives should be related to the size of the capital budget, the size of the operating budget, and the complexity of the real estate tasks. We have also suggested that incentive programs are needed to enhance the performance of top real estate professionals. In addition, we have suggested that new compensation methods need to be used when they become available.

All of the above actions keep the corporation competitive. It is necessary to refer to periodic compensation surveys of real estate executives to be sure that executives in the corporate real estate function are compensated competitively. Huntress Real Estate Executive Search, Inc., conducts an annual compensation survey that is reported in such real estate trade publications as *National Real Estate Investor, Buildings,* and *Shopping Center World.* NACORE International publishes a biennial study of corporate real estate compensation.

New Compensation Methods for Corporate Real Estate Executives

Several new compensation methods, long available in brokerage and development, are gradually being recognized for their importance in corporate real estate. These techniques are

1. Incentive compensation, whereby a significant cash bonus is given to executives who accomplish specific goals

2. Tax shelter programs, where real estate ownership is available on a preferred basis to real estate executives, generating sufficient tax losses to shelter their salaries and, therefore, increase spendable cash, while reducing the pressure for large current salary raises

3. Equity participation, in the form of stock options in public companies or participation in real estate project ownership in private concerns

4. Unbundled fringe-benefit programs, allowing an executive to choose what portion of fringe benefits should be allocated to insurance, health care, pension, employee stock purchase plans, etc., which recognize that executives have different goals and needs at various points in their careers

Corporate real estate has changed dramatically in the past 15 years, but attitudes toward organization and compensation have lagged behind the increasingly complex and sensitive world of corporate asset management. Most firms should fundamentally rethink what they expect of their real property and how they will staff to meet those expectations.

6

Clarifying Responsibilities with Other Departments

James A. Chronley

Senior Vice President, Development, Taco Bell Corporation

Corporations whose principal business is not real estate, but for whom real estate is critical in the conduct of their business, have a great need to coordinate departmental activity carefully. Retail businesses depend upon numerous outlets. Manufacturing, distribution, and financial service companies have similar requirements, though generally for a smaller number of large facilities. Coordination between marketing, construction, operations, finance and accounting, legal services, and real estate units is essential for the successful conduct of business.

Most major corporations develop a strategic plan which optimizes the return on assets employed while minimizing risk and promoting growth. There are three ways to achieve growth. The first is by increasing sales from existing operations. This is referred to as *real growth*. The second is by increasing prices for existing products. The third is by increasing operations, often by increasing locations. The corporate budgeting process

considers all three approaches and looks to the real estate unit to deliver
the new locations required by the third approach.

Growth by new unit development requires varying periods of time,
depending upon the nature of the business; the type of properties to be
acquired, whether leased or purchased; existing resources for new units to
be constructed; local conditions; and the like. Most corporations have a
one-year budget and operating plan. Most real estate activity, especially
construction of new facilities, requires substantially more than one year of
site exploration, identification, approval, permitting, settlement, construction, and opening.

In many major corporations, this process is handled by a two-phase process. The real estate group first delivers all of the sites required in the
current year's plan. Second, real estate develops a pipeline of potential
sites that will provide the actual locations for succeeding years. In a well-
run company, the current year's plan for new locations is virtually fixed at
the beginning of the year. All of the specific locations in the current year's
plan are identified by site and are targeted for a specific opening date during the year. Because of the inevitable unforeseen problems with titles,
permits, soil conditions, and similar factors, there must be some flexibility
in the plan. The plan, however, should be 90 percent fixed.

Development and implementation of the plan requires the appropriate
distribution of responsibilities among the major corporate departments:
marketing, construction, finance and accounting, operations, legal services, and, of course, real estate.

Marketing

Marketing is critical to business success. In retail businesses especially,
there is an absolute requirement that the marketing people plan enough
openings to support anticipated sales and to justify advertising and other
marketing expenses in a given area. The real estate and marketing groups
must keep each other up to date. If, for example, a real estate development
plan called for the opening of a significant number of new units in a new
market during the third quarter of the budget year, marketing would normally plan commercials to be aired in the media to coincide with those unit
openings. If for any reason the timing of the unit openings was changed,
the marketing department would have to be aware of this so that it could
adjust the advertising schedule accordingly.

Most corporations have a target level of marketing effort for each area
in which they advertise. Because advertising dollars are normally allocated
as a percentage of sales dollars, the amount of advertising is the product

of the total number of operating units multiplied by the average unit volume multiplied by the percentage allocated to advertising. Because the cost of media varies dramatically from one marketing area to another, it is essential that the real estate group be familiar with the marketing department's goals and objectives for total new units and marketing expenditures in each market area.

Most businesses monitor the activities of their main competition to better understand the results of their own plans and performance. If a corporation's main competition suddenly becomes very aggressive in specific markets, the marketing people normally are alerted, and they will communicate it to the rest of the organization, including the real estate people, so that appropriate changes in strategy can be made.

Construction

The construction department in most retail organizations operates independently from the real estate group. In most corporations, the architecture and engineering functions either are part of the construction department or report to it. Rarely are construction, architecture and engineering, and real estate in one department. This is unfortunate, because unification of these elements produces optimum communication and cooperation among the functions. In the absence of unification, there is a built-in antagonism between the real estate and construction groups because construction is the last phase of development activity. Construction is usually under greatest pressure to open new units during the current year. Construction must make up the time lost by real estate in securing sites, which is difficult, if not impossible. Most organizations, therefore, adopt a *critical path* that is the time line from the date that a site is secured and approved for development by the corporate managers until the site is opened. A range of 9 to 18 months is not unusual for retail businesses. Unless the construction group has been given a property by the beginning of the second quarter, it is normally not possible for that unit to be opened during the current budget year.

Because the real estate group often operates with two budgets, one for those sites which are to open during the current year and one for those sites which are for succeeding years, a well-coordinated site development process will be sensitive to the needs of both current and succeeding years and will fully communicate the status of performance against objectives in both areas on a regular basis to all departments throughout the year. The most successful vehicle for doing this is a comprehensive report published on a regular basis—monthly or weekly. The important thing is that it be regular and accurate. Accuracy is best achieved by having the data for the report come from the field organizations actually responsible for securing the sites and building the units.

These regular reports should list all units for the current year's operating plan as well as those units to be secured for opening in succeeding years. In addition to identifying each unit, the report should include the exact status and projected dates for permitting, bidding, construction, and opening. Other dates which are important to particular departments should also be included in the report—ground breaking, for example, which triggers equipment delivery scheduling.

Architecture and engineering, whether part of the construction or not, are key functions in the construction process, making certain that the site and building plans for each project are produced in a timely way with minimal need for revision. Most corporations have a comprehensive construction manual that is provided to the architects and engineers to guide them in producing the site and building plans for individual areas. Variations in building requirements are caused by geographic differences. In California, for example, it is necessary to provide building plans that address earthquake hazards. In Florida and the Gulf Coast states, hurricanes are a special problem. In northern climates, snow removal and insulation from the cold must be confronted.

In addition to the climatic conditions, various local zoning and building codes demand special accommodations. These codes establish such things as the number of parking spaces to be provided; dimensions for front, rear, and side yard setbacks; height restrictions; floor area ratios; and specific requirements for signage. The real estate group must thoroughly investigate local requirements for development of the planned site to ensure that the codes will allow what the company intends to build.

One of the most frustrating things that the corporate real estate executive must deal with are sites that are not properly zoned for the corporation's needs. For this author, 30 years of experience in retail site development have taught that only 10 percent of the locations which are not already properly zoned ever receive the zoning variance or change necessary for the proposed nonconforming use. Because the resources necessary to move such a project forward are the same as those for locations which are properly zoned, it does not make good financial sense to work with sites that are improperly zoned. Taco Bell has adopted a policy which precludes pursuing sites that do not have proper zoning. In addition to saving money and avoiding aggravation, this policy helps its public image. The press, unfortunately, is full of examples of major corporations seeking variances for nonconforming development. Most of the reports associated with this type of activity are unfavorable to the corporation and prejudice the company's pursuit of other conforming locations in the communities where zoning changes have been sought. The pursuit of improperly zoned property is simply not worth the risk and the cost involved.

Even when the zoning is favorable to the proposed project, it may never come to fruition. In most retail chains, for example, there is a historic ratio of the total number of properties submitted to top management and the number approved and subsequently opened. For major chains, typically four out of five sites proposed are actually opened. Normally, about 10 percent of the sites proposed by the field organization are rejected by top management because of site quality, financial terms, or physical limitations. An additional 10 percent fail because of title defect, failure to get permits, unsatisfactory soil conditions, inability to take possession because of tenants, and other such problems.

This 20 percent failure rate means that a 20 percent cushion must be built into the process; that is, for every 100 units planned, real estate should produce 120 proposals.

Finance and Accounting

Most corporate financial departments have separate groups to address property taxes, corporate income taxes, and capital planning. The real estate group must work closely with all of them to take advantage of financial opportunities.

One of the major opportunities available to corporations, for example, is the right to exchange property of like value without paying capital gains taxes. When a company has real estate assets that are no longer necessary for the operation of the business and that can be disposed of at a substantial profit, the real estate group should focus its attention on the potential of a tax-free exchange.

Taco Bell recently had the opportunity to sell its former headquarters, which it had outgrown. Because of the escalation in office building values in the market where the facility is located, its market price was about 500 percent of book value. Under prevailing tax laws, it was possible to have the corporation that purchased the former headquarters buy land and building assets elsewhere that Taco Bell needed in order to expand business and to utilize the tax-free mechanism.

Property taxes offer similar opportunities. Property taxes are a cost of doing business that need regular scrutiny to be certain that the corporation is not paying more than its fair share. Unfortunately, many large corporations are absentee taxpayers and are, therefore, not well positioned to protect their interests or monitor tax activity within a given community.

The theory of ad valorem taxes states that like-properties should be similarly assessed. That is not always the practice followed. Most major corporations, therefore, have a group whose function is to monitor real property taxes by comparing assessments in each assessment area to be certain that each property pays only its fair share. For regional and national firms this presents a real challenge. Property taxes differ dramatically from one area to another. There may be as much as a 1000 percent difference, depending upon the quality of the real estate and its location.

The function demanding the closest cooperation between real estate and financial people is budgeting. Once the planning has been completed, the real estate group must address overhead expenses and the capital budget for new locations. Overhead expenses in many corporations are handled either partially or entirely as a capital charge and are amortized together with the cost of land, building, and equipment over the life of the facility. This is a perfectly legitimate and realistic way of handling the overhead budget for new sites, and it is accepted as good accounting practice. Overhead normally includes the cost incurred by the various departments of the company in order to open new locations, for example, salaries and benefits attributable to this activity, travel, and legal fees. A simple formula for spreading the overhead of departments involved in the development of new units is to divide the total costs by the total number of units opened and allocate an equal amount per unit, which is amortized with the rest of the unit's capital cost.

It is essential when budgeting for these overhead dollars, whether they are capitalized or expensed (i.e., written off as incurred), to be certain that the personnel, travel, and outside service costs are fully accounted for.

Overhead expenses plus basic capital costs for land acquisition and construction add up to a lot of money. The real estate group must be certain that it has accurately estimated the number of dollars and when those dollars are needed so that the finance and accounting people are prepared and able to meet that need. In some organizations the funds for new-unit expansion are secured through outside lenders. Failure to keep the finance and accounting people informed can result in unnecessary charges and premiums for emergency funds. Careful monitoring of the process and full communication during the year will ensure that there are few, if any, surprises.

Planning and budgeting for expansion should take place well in advance. It is generally good practice to have the complete operating plan, including the budgets, finally approved and in place by the end of the third quarter preceding the year during which the funds are to be expended. This provides sufficient time to marshal resources and to make any changes necessary to execute the plan.

Operations

Someone once said, "Money will buy new facilities, but money won't run them." It is absolutely essential for the successful conduct of the individual unit that the personnel responsible for its operation be involved in its development. To properly staff a new unit, the operations group must recruit and train the necessary personnel. The real estate and construction group must provide sufficient time for the operations group to do this. The entire process from planning to site selection to construction must have input from operations.

Operations personnel may not have technical expertise in real estate or construction, but they usually are experts at estimating the sales a specific location will generate, because they compare the locational characteristics of a prospective site with other successful sites in the market area. Hence the saying: "If the individual unit is very successful, it is because of superior operations; if it is unsuccessful, it is because of poor real estate."

Legal Services

In most corporations, the preparation or approval of real estate documents is the job of the law department. Ideally, this function reports to the real estate group or is directed by it. Real estate, of course, should not take responsibility for the overall conduct of the corporation's general legal affairs. Depending upon the size of the corporation and its real estate program, there may be anywhere from 1 to 20 people involved in the legal function. If the program is significant, then real estate law becomes very specialized, and a separate group of lawyers may be dedicated to the needs of the real estate unit. Most proposals for the purchase or lease of real estate have some unique terms and conditions which must be reviewed and approved within the context of the corporation's established criteria for making such commitments. This is the function of the real estate lawyer, and it is vital to the orderly and timely conduct of business.

Summary

The real estate executive who has a fully integrated development program that clearly defines objectives and parameters will function best with open lines of communication to all other corporate disciplines. Like most areas of business activity, real estate is dependent upon planning, budgeting, staffing, training, reporting, and following up on the status of activities.

An efficiently operating real estate group will accurately forecast its ability to perform against the current corporate plan and will achieve the required results. It will also be an integral member of the corporate strategic planning group that will guide the corporation in the direction of optimum future growth and profit.

Corporations operate within a specific business sector as well as within the economy as a whole. It is essential that real estate executives be sensitive to their special arena and that they react appropriately as conditions and opportunities change. The way to ensure this is to keep communications open with all departments at all times. Corporate real estate is a team function, requiring complete cooperation and coordination for optimum performance.

7

Choosing Consultants

Cesar J. Chekijian

Vice President, Corporate Real Estate Group,
Manufacturers Hanover Trust Company

Overview

Webster's dictionary defines a consultant as "one who gives professional advice or service." To put the size of the consulting industry in perspective, we could, for all practical purposes, say that almost all service industries fit Webster's definition We have all heard how fast the service sector has grown in the United States since the mid-1960s. It would be safe to say, therefore, in the broadest sense, that we are becoming a nation of consultants, many of us offering advice or service to corporate real estate executives.

The Corporate Real Estate Revolution

Since the early 1970s, real estate in general and corporate real estate specifically have experienced phenomenal growth in values. Between 1970 and 1980 real estate values increased an average 400 percent in the United States; the consumer price index increased only 100 percent. Real estate values also outperformed the gross national product during the 1970s.

Moreover, real estate values as a percentage of total assets of the typical firm doubled between 1970 and 1985, and occupancy costs as a percentage of total revenues of the typical firm doubled during the same period.

This has created opportunities and liabilities for corporate America. The opportunity to redeploy fixed assets with low book values at high market values is offset by the penalty of excessive growth rates in occupancy costs, which have reduced earnings by at least two percentage points from 1970 to 1985 in the typical firm. In 1984, the *Forbes* 500 lost $50 billion of its total revenues of $2.6 trillion to the excessive growth of occupancy costs. These companies, in other words, could have had $190 billion in earnings for 1984 instead of the $140 billion actually recorded. Assuming a price to earnings ratio of 10 to 1, corporate America lost $500 billion of stock market value in 1984 because of the excessive growth of occupancy costs.

During that 15-year period, the corporate real estate profession did not grow proportionately, in either size or sophistication, creating a major opportunity for the consulting industry to fill the void. This brought about substantial additional growth and specialization in corporate real estate consulting.

Corporations, recognizing in the early 1980s the major impact of the real estate revolution of the 1970s, have begun to establish more sophisticated corporate real estate units in-house. These fully staffed departments or subsidiaries often have profit-and-loss responsibilities in addition to meeting the service needs of corporations. They operate like any other business unit of the corporation. This is reducing direct reliance on the consulting industry but certainly not eliminating the need for consultants.

The Need for Consultants

Corporate real estate is as diversified as corporate America itself, providing the physical environments in which the corporation conducts its business. The complexities of anticipating, creating, managing, and divesting of facilities are the responsibility of corporate real estate professionals, whether the need is for a manufacturing plant, an office building, a retail outlet, a research and development center, or a warehouse.

In addition to providing various facilities, corporate real estate units normally operate in several states, if not nationally or internationally, encountering a variety of political, cultural, and economic circumstances. Corporate real estate is a group of individual locations, each with its special characteristics, which require local knowledge, expertise, and capabilities for acquisition, management, and disposition. The local nature of real estate thus often requires the services of a local consultant.

Consulting needs are also determined by the activities in which a particular corporate real estate unit engages. The contemporary corporate real estate unit could include the following functions:

1. Market research and planning
2. Space planning
3. Acquisition and divestitures
4. Legal services
5. Design and construction
6. Property management
7. Property tax evaluation
8. Real estate controllership
9. Real estate finance
10. Real estate investment management
11. Appraisal
12. Strategic real estate planning

The consulting industry has specialists for each of the functions mentioned above.

The Consultant's Role

Corporations without real estate units regularly rely on outside consultants to perform many, if not all, of their real estate tasks. The consultant usually reports to someone in the personnel, controller, law, finance, or facilities department. This is still common practice.

A consultant's relationship with a corporate real estate unit is different, because most, if not all, of the regular real estate functions are performed by the unit. A consultant, therefore, must save time, bring economic advantage, or perform with superior technical skills to be of value to a corporate real estate executive. Here is a description of the consultant's role in each of the dozen major functions of today's corporate real estate organization.

Market research and planning. A retail chain wants to enter a new market, and its corporate real estate people need to know where to locate retail units in that market. A consultant specializing in site selection could provide data about traffic, population, income, and buying habits to promote a proper understanding of the new market.

Space planning.   A corporation needs to determine the five-year office space requirement for its headquarters and several regional operations centers. This would call for an evaluation of the five-year business plans of scores of operating units of the corporation. Unless the corporate real estate unit was staffed to perform this labor-intensive assignment within a reasonable time, which is rarely the case, a consultant with such capabilities should be brought in to perform the task.

Acquisitions and divestitures.   Brokers act as consultants to the corporate real estate unit in most buy-sell and lease transactions. Local knowledge and salesmanship are what the broker-consultant brings to the corporate real estate office.

Legal services.   Local counsel can be most useful in many legal facets of corporate real estate, including appeals for special permits, zoning variances, environmental permits, historical preservation matters, litigation, and the legal aspects of negotiations.

Design and construction.   Extensive use of consultants in this area has been the norm in corporate real estate, where plans are normally generated by outside architectural firms and construction executed by independent general contractors.

Property management.   In-house property management for corporations with many properties distributed over a wide geographic area is nearly impossible. Local or regional property management firms can provide the attention to detail which is essential to good property management and which a central corporate office many miles away simply cannot provide.

Property tax evaluation.   Regular review of assessments is essential to prevent unfair taxation. When properties are scattered around the country or overseas, one central office cannot deal effectively with the various assessing authorities. This requires refined local knowledge of property values, tax laws, and procedures for appeal.

Real estate controllership.   Financial planning, management, and control by advanced management information systems have created a major opportunity for consultants to make a substantial contribution to the corporate real estate field, particularly when corporate mainframe computers cannot provide the software and hardware needed to service corporate real estate.

Real estate finance.   Investment bankers, institutional investors, pension funds, insurance companies, and institutional developers, acting as consultants, have taken corporate real estate finance to Wall Street. With every announcement of a major corporate real estate transaction appears the name of a major Wall Street firm which acted as an adviser to one of the parties in the transaction.

Real estate investment management.   Consultants specializing in redeployment of corporate real estate assets, properties which are underutilized or surplus, are of growing importance. Their job is to see a property not for what it is but for what it could be. They bring vision, initiative, and local knowledge to the disposition problem.

Appraisal.   The determination of property value is essential to real estate transactions. Independent appraisals are the customary means of setting value. Professionally done, they can be relied upon by all parties.

Strategic real estate planning.   Many management consultants specialize in consolidation, decentralization, relocation, organizational planning, and long-range facilities planning. They are specialists at stepping back from day-to-day operations and considering the long view, which is difficult for those operating corporate real estate units to do.

Selecting Consultants

Once the need for outside assistance has been determined, a corporate real estate executive should gather references from any one or a combination of the five primary sources for consultant recommendations:

1. *Direct referrals.*   Start with the consultant files of your own and other departments in your company. Personal references from outside attorneys, accountants, bankers, architects, and other professionals with whom you do business are also reliable, as are references from members of the professional associations to which you belong.

2. *Professional associations.*   Virtually all consultants belong to an association representing their specialty. Your corporate librarian or the reference librarian at your local public library can identify these associations. Failing that, try telephone directory assistance for Washington, D.C., where most associations are headquartered or at least have offices. The objective is to speak with the research department of the association of the given specialty to request the names of the five most appropriate consultants. Also obtain the name of the local association chapter president in the place of the assignment, along with the names of the presidents for two adjoining chapters. Speaking directly with the chapter presidents, discuss in general terms the nature of the assignment. Obtain from them the names of the three most appropriate consultants.

3. *Chamber of commerce.*   By calling state and local chambers of commerce, you will obtain references similar to those available from profes-

sional associations. Foreign chambers of commerce representatives at embassies in Washington or local consulates are good references for international consulting assignments.

4. *State governments.*   State economic development agencies are there to assist corporations seeking to do business in their states. They are a valuable source of consulting references.

5. *Utility companies.*   The business development offices of local public utility companies will often assist in such matters if you are already a customer, could become one, or could affect another customer.

Once a list of about 10 consultants has been generated from these five sources, prepare a matrix to evaluate and eliminate candidates. The top 3 should be interviewed. If the formal interview is satisfactory, solicit from each consultant a written proposal describing schedule, cost, procedure, relevant previous assignments, and client references. Approach the selection of a consultant as if hiring internal staff.

The Consulting Relationship

To assure success in working with consultants, establish good communication. Communication with a consultant should be as close as with internal staff. The responsibility to manage and direct a consultant is no less than it is for internal staff.

Most consultants want to establish lasting relationships with clients. They make their best efforts not only to excel in the technical aspect of an assignment but to demonstrate their dedication to the client, much as a good corporate employee would. That is the incentive for the consultant to continue to excel in subsequent assignments, but the relationship should be tested each time. Many corporations have been shortchanged by relying blindly on relationships established over a period of years.

One *Fortune* 500 company, for example, had a relationship with a property-tax consultant for over 20 years. The consultant firm customarily had all assessment notices mailed directly to its office by the assessing municipalities. The corporate client, relying on a long relationship, felt that everything was under control and that its rights and obligations were professionally monitored. After an overdue review of the situation by the client's corporate real estate unit and two other consulting companies, it was discovered that the corporation had overpaid $1 million a year for many years on its headquarters property taxes alone. An additional $1 million a year in overpayments were made for other properties.

A strong consulting relationship, tested and reaffirmed by superior performance in every assignment, is critical. Lasting relationships with good consultants can produce the same advantages as long-term relationships with corporate employees: experience, institutional memory, and loyalty.

Compensating Consultants

Consultants' compensation should be thought of as part of the overall budget of a given project. The consultant's fee should account for a reasonable percentage of total project cost, like any other hard or soft cost. The corporate real estate executive should try to tailor the fee according to the nature, scope, and characteristics of each project. The consultant should be aware of the overall project budget, whether paid on a retainer, per diem, contingency, or other basis. Where possible, the consultant's compensation should be contingent on the successful completion of the project. Here are some examples:

1. A space-planning consultant could share in the savings from occupancy costs reductions.
2. An energy consultant could be paid a percentage of energy savings generated.
3. A property-management specialist could receive a percentage of gross or net income.
4. A property-tax consultant could be paid a percentage of tax refunds or savings.
5. An investment-management adviser could be compensated on the basis of a percentage of value added to corporate assets.
6. A construction-management consultant could be compensated by a percentage of savings on overall construction costs.
7. Brokers, of course, are normally engaged on a contingency basis, receiving a percentage of a given transaction.

In each example the consultant comes on board at the risk of not getting paid at all if no savings are generated or no value added beyond a base amount established at the start.

Expectations from Consultants

In establishing what is anticipated from a consultant, overstated expectations backfire as often as understated ones. The corporate real estate executive must consider the capabilities of a consultant, regardless of the consultant's self-estimate. A consultant should provide accurate, up-to-date, comprehensive, and unbiased information. A consultant expects clear, reliable, objective, and open directions from the client. A consultant should add something to the process. Corporate real estate clients should ask if a consultant is performing better than they themselves could have performed the task. If not, the relationship should be questioned.

Limitations of Consultants

Do not expect a consultant to understand the firm as well as you do. A consultant is usually brought in to meet a specific need. The client will be held responsible for the consultant's contribution long after the consultant has gone. Also remember that a consultant representing a firm may not be as well received as a corporate employee would. Outsiders may wonder if the consultant actually speaks for the firm. The client must be prepared to back up the consultant.

Striking a Balance

Historically, corporate real estate units have been smaller and less sophisticated than management teams in the real estate industry at large because corporations are not primarily in the real estate business. This does not mean that a corporation should not manage its real estate in a businesslike manner, just like any other unit of the corporation. The expertise gap continues to be filled by the consultant, acting as a knowledge conduit between the corporate real estate unit and the marketplace. In a balanced client relationship, the consultant is one part adviser, one part employee, and one part business partner.

8

Real Property Management Information Systems

Ronald R. Richard

Senior Principal, Management Information Systems,
Laventhol & Horwath

Introduction

Management Information Systems

Corporate real estate management encompasses a variety of facilities: office buildings, shopping centers, industrial parks, multiuse centers, plants, warehouses, manufacturing facilities, sales offices, and laboratories. It also includes real estate held for investment purposes and real estate that a corporation develops in order to realize a profit.

Personnel in a real estate department may be responsible for a number of activities, including property management, construction management, acquisition, divestiture, leasing, site selection, capital budgeting, identification of new investment needs, financial analysis, and record keeping.

A key factor in effective real estate management is reliable information which can be easily accessed and retrieved in a flexible reporting format. In today's marketplace, there are many technological innovations which make the use of automation attractive for corporate real estate management.

Current Technological Perspective

Many system alternatives exist today to provide information to decision makers. Information systems are more valuable to some companies than to others. Value is dependent on the company's business and how astute management is in taking advantage of technology. A company's success with the new information technology depends to a great extent on how comfortable senior management is with it. Depending on the sensitivity with which they are introduced into a company, information systems can either win friends or create enemies. Exposure to the personal computer has sensitized executives to the potential of information processing. The efficient flow of information is now as crucial to a company's success as any other management function.

Placing accurate and timely information in the hands of decision makers is a matter of dollars and cents in all businesses. A database can give executives easy access to information and the ability to analyze it and call up the information they need in the form they want.

Personal Computers.   Microcomputers have become an accepted tool in the business world. The microcomputer can be best characterized as a personal computer which is used by an individual or shared by a small group. Micros can provide built-in user independence and lead to greater individual productivity. Basically, a system consists of the computer and keyboard, a display monitor, storage devices, and usually a printer. The success of microcomputers is based on the following criteria:

- Reasonably priced for the buyer
- Compact enough to fit on a desk top
- Easy to use
- Expandable by the user
- Supported by a variety of software

The initial use of the microcomputer in the office environment has been for local, individualized processing. Users now indicate the need to obtain the data directly from the main computer in the company. This has created the demand for direct communication between the microcomputer at the manager's desk and the host system.

Telecommunications.   The possibility of using a microcomputer to link with mainframe computers, other microcomputers, or remote information databases is an accepted fact. Remote communication between a computer and a database is fairly straightforward.

In addition to a microcomputer and a telephone line, a modem, communications software, and a subscription to an information utility are required. The modem translates digital computer information into telephone signals. The communications software makes the computer function like a communicating terminal. Information utilities, which sell information over phone lines, are becoming a way of life in the modern business office. Information is power, and people in business who possess the best and the latest information are most likely to succeed.

Local-area networks (LAN) provide a flexible way to interconnect microcomputers, share costly computer resources such as high-speed printers, access central data files, and communicate from one computer to another. Networks are very flexible because it is possible to connect just a few or many computers and other devices to one another in a single system. Information travels from one piece of equipment to another over wires or cables under the control of network equipment and programs.

An alternative to local-area networks is private branch exchange (PBX) equipment for interconnecting computers. A PBX is essentially a switch that connects one device to another. Traditionally, PBXs have been used to connect one telephone to another, but they can now do the same thing for computers.

Office Automation. An office automation system is one that permits office personnel to execute functions which include data, word, voice, and image processing by using a single computer network. There are a number of new office automation systems on the market, but no company has integrated every aspect of its office operations. Personal computers have become a catalyst in the integration of office automation systems. The expansion of information technology provides a variety of alternatives for establishing a real property management information system.

Benefits of MIS

Companies have traditionally viewed information systems as tools for operating efficiently. They may also be able to use technology to gain a competitive edge in their corporate real estate management. Information resources can be used to grow in a new area of the real estate business or to transform an existing business into something unique. Executive workstations, based on personal computers or terminals linked to corporate mainframes, allow decision makers to call up a wealth of information from a variety of sources and to analyze it in relatively unstructured ways. Real estate managers can apply these resources to solve problems and identify opportunities in activities ranging from strategic planning to project development, budgeting, real estate portfolio management, and more.

An information system's usefulness is a direct function of the degree to which it affects managerial decisions. A properly focused information system centers attention on those financial and operational factors which real estate managers must directly plan, affect, track, and control to meet their responsibilities effectively. The information allows managers to focus on the key activities which must be performed well in order to be successful in the management of corporate real estate.

Risk of MIS

One risk related to the implementation of a management information system is that the dollar investment may not be recovered. This may occur if users find the system difficult to utilize owing to lack of proper training or design problems. It is not unusual to find a computer system gathering dust because of user resistance.

Numerous headaches can result from an improperly planned and implemented system. Converting information systems to a computer can be very difficult if the office staff, who will be using the equipment, have not been consulted or briefed during the selection process. Some personnel may resist learning how to operate the system for fear of being replaced, losing power, or losing knowledge.

Superficial analysis of the information requirements may result in designing or acquiring a system which is inadequate in meeting the company's real property information needs. Failure to plan properly for future growth or to analyze a system's expandability can result in a system's becoming obsolete prematurely. Dealing with a vendor with marginal financial stability may also result in a system which cannot be maintained or enhanced after the vendor's demise.

Some companies overinvest in their computer system owing to a superficial evaluation of vendor alternatives and a failure to ask enough questions of vendor personnel. This excessive investment may not be recovered over the life of the system. The system may end up costing more than expected, especially if the software is custom-developed. Systems design and development requires many hours of analysis that, if not carefully planned and controlled, can result in costs that exceed the hardware costs.

Many misconceptions exist regarding the acquisition and deployment of computers, in part because of an overemphasis on the simplicity of computer systems and because of the lack of user knowledge about buying a computer. The most frequent misconceptions about buying a computer are the following:

- The computer will arrive at the office ready to plug in and operate.
- The computer will be widely accepted by the staff.
- Computers don't break down because they are solid-state technology.

These misconceptions can also lead to unnecessary risks in the acquisition of a computer system.

All of the above risks can be minimized by conducting a detailed analysis of the company's information requirements prior to purchasing any system.

Management Mandate

The development of a property management system can assist in the realization of management's mandate to achieve profitability, to be competitive, and to continue the growth of the corporation. Real estate asset management controls billions of dollars of fixed assets, which can contribute significantly to a corporation's profitability. The real estate division should be judged on the basis of its contribution to profit performance and it should be directly accountable to top management in a fashion similar to the operating units.

A properly defined database system can provide real estate management with the information required to make essential decisions based on current and accurate data. Financial modeling software allows minimum-risk exploration of project and investment alternatives. Computers can provide timely information on changing conditions in the real estate marketplace, so managers can respond quickly and be competitive.

Major Information Needs

There are a number of information needs in the typical corporate real estate office, but we will focus on only some of the major needs.

Real Property Database

The datebase requirements will depend on the types of real estate a corporation owns, manages, invest in, and develops. At a minimum the database must include an inventory of each facility and parcel of land owned by the corporation with the following data elements for each asset: property name, property address, management company, percentage of ownership, property type, building area, land area, parking spaces, year built, year acquired, number of offices and retail shops, and comments. The database allows for adding a master record for a new property or to modify an existing property master record. Additional records which can be created include a mortgage information record, a depreciation record, and a lease record. The mortgage record provides the following data elements: original principal amount, interest rate, term, start date, payment frequency, periodic payment, debt-service coverage, participation percent and base amount, mortgagee, and type of lender participation. Multiple mortgage records may be present for each property.

The depreciation record includes property name, asset description, original cost, depreciation method, and date placed in service. Lease information should be included in the database with the following elements: property name and address, floor or land area leased, lease term with the beginning and ending dates, lease changes or options, monthly rent, annual rent, common area cost, inflation adjustment, and maximum increase percentage. Where a shopping center or office building is owned, lease information should be available for each tenant similar to that outlined above. Such a database allows for online inquiry to retrieve information by displaying it on a video display terminal or printing it out. Reports can be developed to list out lease expirations by date sequence for corporate leases in various buildings or for tenant leases in buildings owned by the corporation.

Data for each individual lease can be displayed and can also be changed through the video display terminal. Selected leases can be retrieved by indicating specific attributes to control the records selected, for example, by minimum area leased (>1000 square feet), by maximum area leased (<450,000 square feet), by minimum annual rent, and so on. A report can be generated to determine the amount of space for which leases expire year by year, starting with all leases in effect as of a particular year and month. A variety of additional reports can be produced as required. A number of vendors have also developed complete property management systems that provide detailed information and management reports for properties which a corporation has opted to manage for itself.

Database Access

The database described above is normally accessible through a video display terminal. Many vendors also provide tools for more easily retrieving data from a database when there is a need for a special report with selected data. These tools are referred to as *report generators*. They allow the user to specify the criteria for selecting the desired records and also to specify the data elements that should print out on the report, for example, select all leases greater than $2000 per month that will expire in 1987.

A corporation has many databases and it may be useful for the corporate real estate department to have access to some of these databases with the appropriate security clearance. In addition, there are a number of outside databases which can be accessed via a microcomputer and a telephone line. These databases provide access to financial, economic, and real estate data, which can be very helpful to the corporate real estate department.

An online database is a file of information available to anyone who has a computer, communications software, a modem, and a telephone. Online services provide the databases to users who pay a yearly subscription fee to the service or pay a monthly minimum and an hourly access time rate. Five vendors contending in the online business database market are Dialog, The Source, Dow-Jones News/Retrieval, News Net, and CompuServe.

Before deciding whether online databases can be helpful to you, begin by looking at online services in general. The amount of information available online can be overwhelming. How much and what kind of data do you need? Does the service offer only current data or historic, archival data? How many different kinds of data are available? Does the service contain newsletters, periodicals, journals, textbooks, current newspapers, and a news wire? How often are the data updated? How are the data presented? How much will the service cost?

Decision Support Systems

A decision support system is any computer-based system that provides useful assistance to a decision maker. It should improve the effectiveness of decision making. The introduction of personal computers created a fundamental change in the relationship between the accessibility of data, the accessibility to computation, and the decision process.

In the course of daily management activities, the choice of tools to aid in making business decisions must be quite specific. The quantity of information required for individual decisions may depend on the kind of decision that needs to be made. Decision support software must be flexible enough to meet your needs. The most important thing is to know your needs in the first place.

The real value of any decision support activity is often the modeling stage, not the results stage. Besides learning and talking about your business, you start to understand how to make decisions, regardless of what the numbers say.

Decision support software should allow flexibility to respond to unique conditions. Some systems combine graphics, database management, a spreadsheet, and a scheduling capability in the same package. Others can provide applications such as investment analysis, credit analysis, and competitive analysis. One package offers integrated decision support, including report writing, graphics, financial applications, forecasting and statistics, modeling, and database management. Another system includes budgetary planning and control, financial statement forecasts and reports, cash-flow forecasts, and investment analysis.

Spreadsheet Systems

A *spreadsheet* is a matrix of numbers with a set of underlying relationships defined by the user. Spreadsheets are named after the large worksheets with many rows and columns that are commonly used by accountants and analysts. An electronic spreadsheet program puts a columnar paper on your computer screen, dividing it into rows and columns. The rows and columns keep everything neatly lined up, which is very helpful for developing forecasts, projections, and budgets. With a spreadsheet program, you can move the cursor around the screen and type in a number where you want it. Corrections can be made instantly and numbers can be moved around the screen. A simple instruction causes the computer to add it all up. If you change some numbers in any column, the spreadsheet program remembers your instruction and adds the column up again using the new values. If you change one number, the whole sheet changes.

Most spreadsheet programs keep their spreadsheets completely in computer memory and thus are limited by the size of the computer memory. How important that may be to you depends on what you use the spreadsheet program for.

All spreadsheet programs will perform everyday math for you. In addition, they feature built-in formulas and functions that act as shortcuts. There are similar math functions common to virtually all spreadsheet programs, including average, mean, rounding, integer, square root, absolute value, and statistical functions. Some programs offer the financial function net present value, and a few offer internal rate of return and depreciation as built-in functions.

Today a number of vendors offer integrated programs that combine spreadsheet, database manager, and graphics programs all in one. The only way to choose the right spreadsheet program for your use is to compare your needs to the program's abilities. The more elaborate and the more specific your demands, the more research you should do. If you use the spreadsheet or its integrated programs only occasionally, it must be easy to learn and easy to remember, or you will have to relearn the commands every time.

The availability of templates is also an important factor in choosing a spreadsheet package. *Templates* are prewritten spreadsheets that already have everything laid out and all the formulas stored. All you do is fill in the blanks. Templates are handy for standardized operations like real estate investment, construction calculations, competitive bidding analysis, and price estimates. The best-selling and best-established programs have many third-party templates to choose from.

An obvious starting point is to begin by outlining your needs and from there to put the performance trade-offs in perspective. Take a look at what you do. What size project do you typically tackle? What do you want to accomplish, considering the size of the project? Look at the work you expect to put on the computer, especially the size of the spreadsheets and the complexity of what you plan to do. Will you need a lot of built-in functions or statistical formulas? Evaluate the features that will assist you in your projects.

Spreadsheets have become an essential personal computing tool for many users, even those who never imagined themselves being involved in arithmetic projections or analysis. Spreadsheet programs can be of great assistance in the development of budgets for individual real estate properties that are owned and managed by the corporation. These programs can also be used in financial analysis, such as the development of a cash flow forecast or a lease revenue forecast by tenant for individual properties or for all properties on a portfolio and for all properties on all portfolios.

System Alternatives

Several major alternatives exist for the implementation of a real property management information system.

Current In-House System

Most corporations have some form of an installed and operational in-house system. They are usually minicomputers or mainframe computers and are used for accounting applications and production systems, for example, manufacturing production control. It may be possible for the real estate division to computerize its requirements by using an existing system. A disadvantage of this approach may be the inability to have the system installed on a timely basis due to the backlog of other systems which have a higher implementation priority. An assessment should be made of the time frame which is available for implementing the system and evaluating whether it is reasonable in meeting the division's needs.

Time-Sharing Vendor

A time-sharing service offers a wide variety of data-processing applications and other products and services such as specialized programming and consulting. Two key concepts to consider are service and specialization. Most time-sharing companies will provide all the hand-holding necessary to get your applications up and running. The services may include training your staff, furnishing hardware, developing software, and providing other data-processing consulting.

Each vendor will normally select a target market in which to specialize. The company then concentrates its resources in a chosen application and promotes a reputation of expertise in that specialty.

Why use a time-sharing vendor? Some companies prefer not to deal with the problems of ownership and are willing to pay a little more for the peace of mind gained by relying on an outside company to fix whatever goes wrong. Another strong incentive for selecting time sharing is the case of use. A company's in-house facility might be devoted to high-priority processing with little time for other functions such as real estate. Time sharing enables you to buy only as much computing power as you need and to pay only for what you use. It is possible to increase or decrease the size of the system from day to day.

Personal Computers

Personal computers provide users with the ability to process many applications as well as the capability of linking to an in-house system to access the databases available or to tie in via telephone to a time-sharing vendor that has specialized software.

Today the fastest-growing segment in the software industry is the group of companies developing software for microcomputers. This provides a wider range of application programs to choose from. The decline in cost versus the increase in performance and capacity also makes microcomputers a very attractive alternative.

Evaluation of System Alternatives

Experience shows that there is a logical approach that should be followed to minimize the risks in evaluating and selecting system alternatives. Automation cannot be rushed. When you are investigating different systems, some vendors will probably lead you to believe that their system can be implemented in less time than is realistic. The length of the implementation process cannot be determined until the extent of your data-processing project and the impact on your current method of operations are known.

In implementing a data-processing system, the corporation and the vendor do not always consider the interfacing of existing manual systems along with the development of modifications to existing procedures and methods of operating. There is also the need to train the various support personnel throughout the organization.

User Requirements Definition

In analyzing user requirements it is important to distinguish unneeded frills from vital functions. The needs for the system should be defined in terms of required applications, desired applications that might be processed in the future, and potential applications that may come along later. More emphasis should be placed on the current required needs than on uncertain future needs. The first step for establishing the user requirements is to complete a detailed definition of the proposed system. This description thoroughly covers the functions to be performed, the outputs to be produced, and the inputs required by the new system. The goal is to describe user needs to the point that there can be no mistaking what features the new system should include. All functions involved in the new system should be completely identified in terms of both their manual and automated components.

After the description of functions to be performed by the system is complete, the definition of system outputs is addressed. There should be a description of every key report that should be produced by the system to fulfill user needs. This definition should include estimates of the frequency of the reports and the reports' purposes in the organization. A specification should be made of the exact manner in which all computer inputs must interface with your existing procedures, forms, and data files.

Conceptual Design

Once the current system has been reviewed, the information needs identified, and the requirements for the new system defined, a conceptual design can be created. The conceptual design consolidates all the data previously gathered and identifies the relative priorities of the information needs. Alternative methods of operation are explored in the form of new system approaches. Analysis of the alternatives will consider existing in-house computer systems, time-sharing systems, and microcomputers. Preliminary cost estimates should be obtained from vendors to compare the various alternative approaches being considered.

Cost-Benefit Analysis

In general, a detailed cost-benefit analysis should be performed only when you are not convinced that a computer system is needed at all or when the selection of the best alternative is not clear. The analysis is basically a comparison of the estimated costs and benefits of the new system with the costs and benefits of the old system or another alternative. Both tangible and intangible costs and benefits should be analyzed and their impacts appraised. The benefits of the new system should not be exaggerated. It is important to be as realistic as possible about both costs and benefits. Only major areas of change should be analyzed for the costs and benefits.

Vendor Selection—Prepare
Request for Proposal

A request for proposal (RFP) should be developed and sent to a number of qualified vendors. The vendors will be requested to submit proposals to provide hardware, software, training, documentation, and implementation assistance. By specifying your requirements in a formal, binding document, you will have greater assurance that all of the vendors uniformly understand your requirements. Furthermore, because all of the vendor proposals will be in the format specified in the RFP, the evaluation process will be facilitated. In addition, the RFP can, and should, be included as an attachment to your contract with the vendor selected. This will provide a reference in case any dispute arises concerning the functional capabilities of the vendor's system.

The RFP should include

1. Technical specifications
    a. System overview
    b. Application description
    c. Transaction volumes
2. Equipment requirements
    a. Expandability
    b. Compatibility
3. Conversion requirements
    a. Program conversion
    b. File conversion
4. Education and training requirements
5. Documentation requirements
6. Hardware and software maintenance
7. Required proposal format for submission

Evaluate Vendor Proposals.   Each vendor's proposal should be reviewed to assure adherence to the RFP. The following selection criteria can then be applied:

1. Can various application packages from a specific vendor talk to each other without vendor-supplied interface modules? Can the software communicate to software developed in-house or by other vendors via intelligent, vendor-supplied interface software?

2. Can the system be easily and inexpensively expanded to handle additional processing work loads as your growth might require?

3. Is assistance provided for the training of existing personnel in the operation of the system?

4. Is the security of files and applications adequate to protect confidential information?

5. Is hardware and software maintenance available and reliable?

6. Are there positive user references from other customers regarding the proposed system?

7. What are the costs of the proposed hardware and software?

8. Is the user documentation complete, clear, concise, accurate, well-organized, and easy to use?

9. What is the efficiency and reliability of back-up procedures for master files to ensure adequate recovery capability?

10. What is the financial stability of the vendor?

If the vendor is evaluated in accordance with the above criteria, the likelihood of reaching the right decision will be greatly increased and the selection process will be significantly less cumbersome.

Negotiate a Contract.   The vendor's contract should be reviewed carefully. Typically there is a hardware-software purchase agreement and a separate maintenance agreement. If the package requires modification or if custom development is needed, a software development contract may be added.

The supplier may offer more favorable terms if that is what it takes to land your account. The contract should clearly define the vendor's pricing structure, charges for all additional products and services, hours of service availability, termination provisions, and similar stipulations. If you are not completely satisfied with the standard contract terms, ask the supplier to amend them. Negotiate a payment schedule based upon the vendor's performing against the established implementation timetable.

Implementation

Planning

The vendor should develop a detailed implementation plan covering the installation of hardware, converting the files, modifying packages, and training personnel. The approach for the phasing in of all applications should also be outlined in order to plan for the scheduling of necessary resources. The plan should be monitored on a weekly basis to verify that the vendor is meeting its commitments. Regular status meetings should be held with the vendor to discuss progress, problems, and actions that must be taken to keep the project moving.

Design of Software and Database

If the software requires any modifications, the application specifications must be reviewed and finalized with the vendor. The vendor's detailed design of the programs must also be accepted before any programming takes place.

Emphasis must also be given to the design of the database for the system. The importance of careful review of the vendor's documentation cannot be overemphasized.

The vendor should also develop a conversion plan, identifying conversion programs, manual conversion work, and personnel needs. Additional planning should be done to develop training plans, schedules, a systems test plan, the site preparation plan, and a plan covering when the hardware and software installation are to take place.

Installation

This entails physical installation of all the hardware and software packages. The vendor's testing should not be relied on exclusively. You should prepare some test data. If any hardware does not work properly after a reasonable period of testing and maintenance, the vendor must replace it. The hardware should not be paid for until the system passes acceptance testing.

Training

User controls and procedures are developed with the aim of ensuring precise, accurate entry and maintenance of data in the system. These procedures serve as control mechanisms, dictating the handling of data at both the input and output stages. These controls assure that proper processing is performed at the appropriate time, that accuracy is maintained, and that access to the system is restricted to authorized users.

The vendor should conduct the actual training sessions for the real estate division personnel. The training is very important in developing the comfort level of the personnel who will be using the system day after day.

Final System Testing

The importance of this testing cannot be overestimated. Every aspect of the system must be checked to ensure that it will perform under realistic conditions. Manual and automated components of the system are tested by application areas. Control totals should be carefully checked. At the conclusion of the testing you must be satisfied that the system is sound and that your personnel have had sufficient training.

Conclusion

The evaluation and implementation procedures outlined above are very thorough and are designed to assist you through a cumbersome and risky process. All procedures are not applied in every installation of a computer system. Their use is dependent on the size, cost, and complexity of the system to be installed. Many of the tasks are valid in each system selection, but the level of effort may need to be scaled down when appropriate.

The management of corporate real estate continues to grow in complexity, and there are ever-increasing demands for information that is accurate and timely. Development of a real property management information system is essential in today's competitive environment. Our current technology continues to make automation more attractive and more economical for the real estate division of a corporation.

PART 2
Operations

9

Finance and Budget Analysis

Norman D. Holst

Vice President, Corporate Real Estate, Commerce Bancshares, Inc.

Have you ever had a tenant suddenly move out, leaving only the message "Talk to my lawyer"? Have you ever had a contractor fail to perform owing to financial difficulties? Have you ever been in negotiations where a knowledge of the other side's financial strengths or weaknesses could have made a major difference in how you approached the transaction? Have you ever had a proposal that you felt was an excellent opportunity for your corporation turned down by senior management because they apparently did not understand its financial impact?

If any of the above has happened to you, a better understanding of corporate finance might have avoided the problem. An understanding of corporate finance is important to the corporate real estate executive for several reasons. The corporate real estate executive makes decisions daily on the basis of a conception of the financial condition of the company, the financial conditions of other firms, and the overall financial condition of the economy. If you do not understand the basics of finance, it is impossible to understand your company, your industry, and your competition. You will not be able to understand the goals and objectives of your firm, which are normally measured in financial terms. Finally, knowledge of corporate finance is essential if you are to communicate with senior management, especially senior financial management.

The corporate decision to acquire or dispose of real estate is essentially an investment decision. As such, the corporate decision makers view an investment in real estate as they view other investments. A corporation has limited financial resources, and the decision makers must compare real estate investments with alternatives, using the same criteria to measure the potential return. If the financial planners and decision makers are to understand the benefits of a particular real estate proposal, the measurement criteria must be stated in a form familiar to them.

The purpose of this essay is to familiarize the corporate real estate executive with the goals and objectives of financial management and analysis which may be helpful in handling day-to-day responsibilities and to demonstrate ways to better communicate with financial management and the decision makers of the firm.

Formulating Financial Objectives

The financial management of each firm, regardless of its legal structure, is normally charged with achieving two objectives: (1) maximizing the value of the firm in the marketplace, and (2) managing the cash flow to the maximum benefit of the firm.

Financial management is responsible for advising the decision makers on the critical financial decisions faced by every firm. What volume of funds will be available and how should they be committed to maximize return? How will the firm obtain necessary funds for operations and investments? How can the firm best maximize its profits from its existing and proposed commitments of funds?

Issues of Maximizing Value

These decisions are made primarily by looking for ways to maximize return on investment and minimize cost. Minimization of cost includes budget items such as personnel, marketing expense, operating expense, and the cost of capital, which is the interest rate paid for borrowed funds. The cost of capital becomes critically important to the corporate real estate executive because it is the primary measurement against which all investment proposals are measured. A proposal must be shown to return a minimum on the cost of capital or be rejected. The return on investment of a project will also be measured by the return on the firm's alternative investments. In other words, if the firm is earning an average of 4 percentage points above its cost of capital in its current investment portfolio, it will most likely not make a decision to invest in a real estate venture which shows only a 2 percent margin.

In attempting to maximize the value of the firm in the marketplace, the corporate decision makers are primarily concerned with the value which the financial markets—the stock market, the bond market, institutional lenders—place upon the financial condition of the company. Corporate decision makers, especially financial managers, are extremely interested in any decision which impacts on overall financial condition.

Corporate officers charged with the responsibility of maximizing the value of the firm have numerous tools with which they can work to accomplish their task. The dividend policy of publicly traded firms is one of the most important factors in influencing its stock price. The price of a firm's stock is theoretically the present value of the future expected dividends. Dividends are that portion of a firm's earnings returned to the stockholders in cash and/or additional stock. A firm must choose between reinvesting earnings in additional earning assets in order to gain greater earnings in the future or paying its earnings in dividends. When a firm makes payment of a cash dividend on a regular basis, the investment community will generally pay a premium to obtain this stock because of the lowered risk in receiving income from investment. These dividends also help to stabilize, or cause appreciation in, the stock price. The consistent payment of cash dividends also helps the firm reduce its overall capital cost by making bonds more salable in the marketplace to raise capital through debt.

Investor Measurement of Value

Because the key to enhanced value of a publicly traded firm is the underlying value of the stock price, corporate financial management closely watches several important ratios of its firms' finances to ensure that the marketplace has a clear picture of the firm's financial condition. Financial management is guided by three objectives:

1. To maximize profits by maximizing the return on investment in the firm.

2. To determine the present cash position of the firm and plan for future cash needs.

3. To maintain a financial condition that is favorable to the criteria set by present and future suppliers of money. In looking at these criteria, it

must be remembered that creditors or lenders have one set of criteria and investors another.

The investment community will look at the following financial statistics in evaluating the firm's financial conditions.

1. *Dividend payout ratio.*   The annual dividend per share paid by the company divided by the total earnings per share of the company, indicating the percentage of earnings a company is returning to its investors.

2. *Book value per share.*   The ratio of the equity of the holders of common stock or the net worth of the company divided by the number of shares outstanding, indicating if the liquidated assets of the company will return the dollars invested in the shares of the company.

3. *Earnings per share.*   The net earnings of the company divided by the number of shares outstanding, indicating the percentage appreciation or increase in equity which the investor can anticipate.

4. *Price-earnings ratio.*   The ratio of the market price per share divided by the earnings per share, indicating the multiple which the market is willing to pay for the earnings of that firm.

5. *Capitalization rate.*   The reciprocal of the price-earnings ratio or the earnings per share of the firm divided by the market price, indicating the rate of return on the investment in the stock demanded by the market at a particular time.

6. *Dividend yield.*   The ratio of the dividend per share divided by the market price, indicating the rate of return on the investment in the stock which an individual investor can expect to receive.

Managing Cash Flow

Cash flow is defined as the net income of the firm plus the depreciation of the firm's assets. Depreciation is added back to the net income because it is a noncash expense. Therefore, cash flow is the net number of dollars flowing into the firm during the accounting period. This represents the funds which are available to the firm to pay dividends, invest in new assets, upgrade old assets, or invest in alternatives such as treasury stock. Cash flow is important to the firm's financial management because it measures the working capital available to accomplish other objectives. Cash flow is extremely important to firms interested in real estate. The depreciation techniques which are provided under the current tax regulations allow real estate improvements to be depreciated before the end of the useful life of the asset is reached. This creates additional cash flow, or working capital, with which the firm can operate. On the other hand, it does result in the firm's reporting lower earnings because of the higher depreciation write-offs. It is this "good-news-bad-news" situation which causes many financial managers and corporate decision makers to object to substantial investments in real estate. The firm's financial management has other tools with which to manage cash flow.

Increasing Cash Flow by Obtaining Additional Capital

Occasionally, the firm will need additional cash in the form of capital. The firm at this point must make one of several choices concerning how this capital will be obtained.

All financing is done by either renting, leasing, or buying additional funds. Rented money is usually a short-term loan, but it can be long-term, using existing assets as collateral. Leasing is like renting money, but debentures or bonds of the firm are issued in place of specific asset collateral. Buying money essentially consists of selling shares of ownership or stock in the firm.

There are advantages and disadvantages of each form of financing. For instance, debt financing usually means there is no dilution of ownership. However, if the firm is unable to repay the debt, there is the possibility of loss of management control. There is a tax advantage in that the interest payments are deductible from the income of the firm. The major disadvantage of debt financing is that interest must be repaid; therefore, the use of cash for other purposes is limited. Also, a firm extends a portion of its credit or borrowing power, thereby limiting its ability to borrow in the future until the debt is repaid, and collateral agreements may limit the use of certain assets of the firm until the loan is repaid.

Equity financing, on the other hand, usually results in a dilution or partial loss of ownership by current owners. On the positive side, there is not interest or principal repayment; therefore, cash flow is not encumbered against future needs, nor will there be any encumbrances on the assets of the firm if future loans are needed.

Cost of Capital

The key to managing the acquisition of additional cash flow or capital is the management of the cost of capital. In most firms there are numerous sources of capital, each of which has an individual cost. These sources include various types of debt, preferred stock, common stock, and retained earnings. The importance of the cost of capital to the corporate real estate executive is that it is the *hurdle rate,* or minimum rate of return, which is acceptable for a proposed project. If the expected rate of return on a real estate project is below this hurdle rate, the firm would normally decide to invest its money in a higher returning project or not to borrow money in the first place. While the hurdle rate is the minimum rate by which a new project may be measured, in most firms there is an additional markup added to the cost of capital to justify the risk in the project. In general, the rule for proposed projects is that they will not be undertaken unless the discounted cash flow exceeds the cost of capital by the necessary margin to reward the firm for its risk. Moreover, the net present value of the cash flowing in from the project must be greater than the present value of the cash flowing out, using the same discount rate.

Using Business Cycle Indicators

One additional set of tools used by corporate financial management that should also be familiar to the corporate real estate executive is business cycle indicators for anticipating inflation, recession, and changes in interest cost. The business cycle indicators that corporate decision makers use project the future of the economy or some specific segment of it. There are three types of business indicators, each of which has certain firms or industries most closely synchronized with it. First, *leading business indicators* normally indicate the end of an economic downward trend and the start of an upward trend by their reversal in direction. They consist of the number of new business incorporations, new orders for industrial goods, industrial stock prices, wholesale prices of basic commodities, commercial and industrial construction, residential construction, length of the average workweek, and the business failure rate. Second, *coincidental business indicators* normally confirm trends in the economy by changing direction later in the cycle than the leading indicators. These coincidental business cycle indicators include manufacturing production, nonagricultural employment, unemployment, bank deposits, freight car loadings, wholesale prices, corporate profits, and gross national product. Finally, the *business laggers* are those indicators that confirm the last phase of a business cycle and quite often signal a reversal in trends. These include personal income, retail sales, consumer-installment debt, bank interest rates on loans, and manufacturing investment in new plant and equipment.

Other important indicators of future economic activity, interest rates, and inflation are the monetary policies of the U.S. Treasury and the Federal Reserve System. Often, the actions of the Federal Reserve and the Treasury Department have a major impact on interest rates and the availability of credit. The Federal Reserve and the Treasury control the supply of money, and, therefore, the cost of money, by increasing or decreasing the rediscount rate at which the Federal Reserve loans money to its member banks and by buying or selling treasury obligations.

Importance of Credit

The ability of governments, commercial enterprises, and consumers to borrow money makes it possible to finance major projects, underwrite deficit spending, and maintain adequate cash in spite of an erratic revenue stream. Commercial enterprise can finance expansion. The consumer can finance purchases as needed or desired.

During any one time period, the economy creates only so much new capital from business and consumer savings, from reinvestment, and from expansion of the money supply. The demand for this new capital comes from three sources: government borrowing to finance deficit spending and cash flow, business borrowing to finance working capital and planned expansion, and consumer borrowing to finance new purchases. Given that there is only so much available capital in the marketplace at any one given time, the volume of these combined demands brings the law of supply and demand into play on interest rates. As the available capital is absorbed by borrowers, the remaining dollars available demand a higher price and interest rates rise. This seems to be particularly true when the government enters the marketplace to borrow heavily to finance its operations.

Economic conditions in general can also have an impact on the credit supply and demand and, therefore, on interest rates. Economic conditions are the real and perceived economic situations in which each borrower lives. Collectively, this atmosphere creates the overall economic condition. If the majority sees falling sales and declining profits, then recession and retrenchment may indeed be around the corner. Demand for credit will disappear and interest rates may fall. On the other hand, rising sales, prices, and profits can create an optimistic atmosphere, creating additional demand for credit, resulting in higher interest rates.

The decisions of the firm's senior management are greatly influenced by the credit market. Obviously, the cost of capital to the firm is affected by the market price of credit. Investors as a group have the ability to influence public opinion about economic expectations. If the investment community has expectations of economic opportunity, they may well demand credit to make additional investments, thereby bidding up the price of the firm's stock. This in turn influences how the firm sees itself and how it makes capital investment decisions.

How All This Relates to Corporate Real Estate

If you have made it this far, you are probably wondering what all of this has to do with managing corporate real estate. The purpose of this background material is to introduce the corporate real estate executive to the complexity of corporate finance and to the issues faced on a daily basis by the chief financial officer and senior management of the firm. If the corporate real estate executive has even an introductory understanding of the issues involved in corporate finance, the job of communicating the financial needs of corporate real estate will be easier. Moreover, this introduction is prerequisite to understanding the balance of this essay, in which hands-on applications of financial analysis to the balance sheet and income statement of the company are discussed. Capital budgeting will also be examined.

The Balance Sheet

Financial information about a firm is contained in two basic formats. The first, the balance sheet, shows the value of the firm's assets and the claims against those assets at a specific time. The assets are normally listed from top to bottom in order of decreasing liquidity. The top group of assets, labeled "current assets," includes cash, marketable securities, accounts receivable, and inventories, which are normally convertible to cash within one year. The bottom portion of this listing is normally called "fixed assets" and contains such items as plant, equipment, and other long-term investments, which normally could not be converted into cash within one year. The liabilities and stockholders' equity portion of the balance sheet is arranged similarly. The current liabilities are those which are due within one year and include such items as accounts payable, accrued expenses, and short-term borrowings. The balance of the liability portion of the balance sheet contains long-term debt, which is to be paid off beyond one year, and a statement of the stockholders' investment or equity in the company.

Exhibit 9.1

XYZ FURNITURE MANUFACTURING COMPANY
Balance Sheet, Year End 19XX
(in millions)

Assets	19XX	19XO
Current		
Cash and short-term investments	$ 11.2	$ 8.3
Receivables	23.4	22.8
Inventories	22.2	21.3
Prepaid Expense and other current assets	2.9	1.9
Total current assets	$ 59.7	$ 54.3
Fixed		
Plant and equipment	38.3	38.6
Other real estate	6.7	5.6
Investment in affiliate co.	.9	.5
Other assets	1.4	1.5
Total assets	$107.0	$100.5

Liabilities and shareholders' equity		
Current liabilities		
Accounts payable and accrued expenses	$ 24.7	$ 18.9
Short-term borrowings	1.6	3.5
Income taxes	1.3	3.4
Total current liabilities	$ 27.6	$ 25.8
Long-term debt	23.2	21.8
Stockholders' equity	56.2	52.9
Total liabilities and stockholders' equity	$107.0	$100.5

The Income Statement

The second financial statement for analyzing the firm is the income statement, which shows the income for a specific period of time. This statement contains figures on net sales minus the cost of goods sold, yielding a gross profit figure. From this is subtracted general and administrative expenses to yield the operating income of the firm. Interest expense is subtracted from operating income to obtain the income before taxes. Income taxes are subtracted to yield the net income of the firm.

A firm can provide several types of financial statements. The most acceptable type of statement is one prepared by a certified public accountant with an opinion letter and footnotes attesting to its reliability and value. Other types of statements which may be presented are unaudited statements, usually prepared with no representation of accuracy or reliability, and interim statements, which are usually prepared in-house. Finally, some firms, especially very small operations, may use an "estimated" statement.

Exhibit 9.2

XYZ FURNITURE MANUFACTURING COMPANY
Income Statement for the Year 19XX
(in millions)

	19XX	19XO
Net sales	$198.4	$176.3
Less: Cost of goods sold	141.2	121.8
Gross profit	$ 57.2	$ 54.5
Less: General and administrative expense	40.1	38.4
Operating income	$ 17.1	$ 16.1
Less: Interest expense	1.6	1.6
Income before income taxes	15.5	14.5
Less: Income taxes	7.0	6.6
Net income	$ 8.5	7.9

The examples shown here are greatly simplified versions of what may be presented for evaluation. Different industries use different terminology, and individual accountants have different methods of presentation, but they should follow generally accepted accounting principles.

Ratio Analysis

While the information in these statements is useful in analyzing the firm's financial condition, the tool used to make them more meaningful is *ratio analysis,* a standardized series of calculations developed to show relationships among the various items on the balance sheet and income statement. By developing these ratios and comparing them to past performances of the same firm and to industry standards, you can get a much clearer picture of the firm's financial situation.

With the data from the balance sheet and income statement in hand, you can calculate an infinite number of ratios—some meaningful, some worthless. For corporate real estate executives, ratio analysis can answer several questions: Can this prospective tenant meet the short-term obligations of a lease? Does this prospective supplier have the appropriate working capital to finance the manufacturing of the goods you are ordering? How efficiently does this firm manage the assets under its control? How heavily in debt is this potential joint-venture partner? Is the profitability of this potential acquisition reasonable in light of the investment which the current owners have in it?

Each of these questions was phrased to introduce one of the classifications of ratios to be discussed:

1. *Liquidity*—measures the firm's ability to meet short-term obligations.
2. *Quality of working capital*—measures the true availability of working capital to the firm.
3. *Efficiency of management*—measures the ability of that firm's management to handle the resources at its disposal.
4. *Debt or leveraging*—measures the extent of debt used in financing the firm.
5. *Profitability*—measures the firm's ability to produce an adequate return on investment.

As each of the ratios is explained, an example of how the ratio is calculated will be shown using the XYZ Furniture Manufacturing Company. The ratio will be compared to an industry ratio for manufacturers of wood furniture, drawn from the annual-statement studies published by Robert Morris and Associates, Philadelphia, Pennsylvania.

Liquidity Ratios

The *current ratio* is used to indicate the ability of the firm to meet its day-to-day obligations. This ratio matches the liquid assets of the firm with the short-term obligations of the firm to show how many times those short-term obligations are covered by assets which could be converted into cash in a short period of time. This ratio, which is calculated by dividing current assets by current liabilities, also measures a margin of safety provided for paying current debts. The ratio is a measure of quantity, not quality. Therefore, you need additional information about the components of the assets, such as the accounts receivable and inventory, in order to draw reliable conclusions.

$$\text{Current ratio} = \frac{\text{current assets}}{\text{current liabilities}} = \frac{59.7}{27.6} = 2.2$$

industry standard $= 2.4$

The second liquidity ratio is the *quick ratio* or *asset test ratio*. Its purpose is to provide a measure of the quality of the firm's ability to pay off its short-term obligations by eliminating the firm's inventory from the calculation.

$$\text{Quick ratio} = \frac{\text{current assets} - \text{inventory}}{\text{current liabilities}} = \frac{37.5}{27.6} = 1.4$$

industry standard $= 1.2$

These two ratios indicate that our mythical firm is reasonably close to industry standards in liquidity of assets and has the ability to pay off its short-term obligations from its own resources. The firm could liquidate its current assets for only 46 percent of book value and still pay off its current liabilities. In addition, the quick ratio indicates that the firm has the ability to liquidate its current assets minus its inventory for 71 percent of book value and still pay off its current liabilities.

Keep in mind that industry standards are nothing more than the average of a group of firms in that industry. It is not a magic number that guarantees a firm's financial stability. It is to be used only for comparison purposes. If a firm's ratio varies significantly from the industry standard, you should check further to determine the cause. It may well be that the firm is exceptionally well managed and does not need to maintain ratios near the industry standard.

Working Capital Ratios

Working capital is defined as current assets minus current liabilities. The working capital of a firm is the net funds which the firm has available for day-to-day operations and for additional investments without adding additional capital.

While the working capital ratios do not have comparable industry standards, they are important because they give an indication of the quality of the funds available in the firm to meet day-to-day obligations. For the XYZ Furniture Manufacturing Company, the working capital would be calculated as follows:

Working capital $=$ current assets $-$ current liabilities

$$= 59.7 - 27.6 = 32.1$$

The *ratio of inventory to working capital* measures the dependence of the firm on selling its inventory in order to generate working capital. Because inventory is often a large item on the balance sheet, it is important to know the quality of that inventory. The value of an inventory can change drastically as styles change, obsolescence takes place, deterioration occurs, consumer preferences change, or theft or other losses occur. A change in the value of the inventory can drastically reduce, or even eliminate, working capital if a firm depends too much on inventory as a major source of its working capital.

$$\frac{\text{Inventory}}{\text{Working capital}} = \frac{22.2}{32.1} = 69\%$$

The ratio of accounts receivable to working capital measures the dependence of the firm on its accounts receivable to generate working capital.

$$\frac{\text{Accounts receivable}}{\text{Working capital}} = \frac{23.4}{32.1} = 73\%$$

Again, the quality of the receivables is the key to this ratio. The age of outstanding receivables is critical. You also need to know how diversified the receivables are. Do they represent a small group of firms or are they widespread? Also of interest is whether or not the firm is in a seasonal business. Do they receive a large percentage of their cash during one time of year?

The *ratio of long-term liabilities to working capital* indicates whether or not the borrowings of the firm have been used to replenish working capital or to finance fixed-asset acquisition. This ratio indicates the ability of the firm to borrow in the future. A high percentage indicates the firm may have problems borrowing, while a low percentage indicates the firm should have the ability to borrow additional funds.

$$\frac{\text{Long-term liabilities}}{\text{Working capital}} = \frac{23.2}{32.1} = 72\%$$

This ratio also brings to your attention the existence of long-term debt. Remember that unless long-term debt can be refunded indefinitely from profits, working capital eventually must be reduced to repay the debt.

Efficiency Ratios

Efficiency ratios indicate the ability of a firm's management to use resources under its control. The ratio of net sales to net fixed assets measures the efficiency with which a company utilizes its investment in land, plant, and equipment. A low ratio indicates poor utilization, overcapacity, recent expansion of plant and equipment for future needs, or inadequate sales volume to support the investment. A high ratio indicates sales beyond the production capacity of the firm or that the firm leases a high percentage of its plant and equipment.

$$\frac{\text{Net sales}}{\text{Net fixed assets}} = \frac{198.4}{38.3} = 5.2$$

Inventory turnover is calculated by dividing net sales by inventory. This ratio measures the effectiveness of the firm in marketing its product. Generally, the higher the ratio, the better the condition of the firm. A high ratio, however, can indicate an inadequate inventory, but not for very long, because the ratio will fall rapidly as sales decline when the firm cannot deliver its product. A low ratio usually indicates an inventory or sales problem. This ratio is also a measure of the quality of the inventory in the working capital.

$$\text{Inventory turnover} = \frac{\text{net sales}}{\text{inventory}} = \frac{198.4}{22.2} = 8.9$$

Industry standard = 6.0

The last efficiency ratio to be considered is the *ratio of net sales to total assets*. This ratio measures the utilization of all assets of the company in generating sales. A high ratio usually indicates the company is doing an outstanding job of managing its assets, while a low ratio may indicate that the sales revenues of the firm do not justify the investment in assets.

$$\frac{\text{Net sales}}{\text{Total assets}} = \frac{198.4}{107.0} = 1.8$$

Industry standard = 1.9

Debt or Leveraging Ratios

Debt or leveraging ratios measure the extent to which the investment in the firm is financed by borrowed capital. These ratios indicate whether the creditors or equity owners bear the largest risk of investment in the firm, whether the equity owners are in a strong ownership position or have a silent "partner" in their creditors, and if the firm has the ability to repay its debt from its current operations.

The *ratio of total debt to net worth* measures the owner's interest in the firm versus the interest of the creditors. Ratios lower than the industry standard denote strong ownership and freedom of action for management. Ratios higher than the standard generally indicate weaker management and more influence by creditors on the firm. Creditors can limit the freedom of management by imposing strict payoff schedules and limiting the use of collateral.

$$\frac{\text{Total debt}}{\text{Net worth}} = \frac{50.8}{56.2} = 90.4\%$$

Industry standard = 71.4%

The *net sales to net worth ratio* is known as the *trading or leverage ratio.* This calculation measures the extent to which a firm's sales are supported by investment capital. A high ratio can indicate an unduly large debt. On the other hand, a low ratio usually indicates low sales or inefficient use of equity investment.

$$\frac{\text{Net sales}}{\text{Net worth}} = \frac{198.4}{56.2} = 3.5$$

Industry standard = 3.3

The *debt ratio or ratio of total debt to total assets* measures the percentage of funds borrowed to support the assets of the company. A high ratio indicates that the firm may have trouble borrowing additional funds in the future and that the firm is running the risk of large losses if the rate of return on investment drops below the cost of capital. In a highly leveraged situation, as long as the firm can earn more on the investment than it costs to obtain the funds, the earnings of the firm are increased by the percentage spread between the return on investment and the cost of capital. The payment of interest and return of principal must be financed from working capital or stockholders' equity in the firm.

$$\text{Debt ratio} = \frac{\text{total debt}}{\text{total assets}} = \frac{50.8}{107.0} = 47.5\%$$

Industry average = 43.1%

The final ratio in this category is the *ratio of net profit before taxes to interest expense,* a measure of the firm's ability to meet its debt obligations. It also indicates the degree to which the firm's earnings can fall without the firm being unable to meet its annual interest costs.

$$\frac{\text{Net income before income taxes}}{\text{Interest expense}} = \frac{15.5}{1.6} = 9.7$$

Industry standard = 6.3

Profitability Ratios

Measures of profitability are *return on equity, return on assets,* and *profit margin.* These three ratios are also measures of the effectiveness of management. All of the ratios discussed above give interesting and useful information, but profitability ratios are the final test.

The *return on equity ratio or net profit divided by net worth* measures the profit return on investment or the reward for the risk of ownership to the shareholders. It also measures the ability of the firm to pay dividends as well as to retain earnings for future growth. If the firm is highly leveraged with borrowed capital or has a very low net worth, the picture of success can be greatly distorted by this ratio.

$$\text{Return on equity} = \frac{\text{net profit}}{\text{net worth}} = \frac{8.5}{56.2} = 15.1\%$$

Industry standard = 19.4%

The *return on assets ratio* measures the return on the total investment in the firm.

$$\text{Return on assets} = \frac{\text{net profit}}{\text{total assets}} = \frac{8.5}{107.0} = 7.9\%$$

Industry standard = 10.8%

The *profit margin or ratio of net profits to net sales* measures the success of the firm in reaching its fundamental goal of realizing a profit. The resulting ratio is the percentage of each sales dollar the firm recognizes as profit. It is essential that this ratio be compared with industry standards in order to have any usefulness.

$$\text{Profit margin} = \frac{\text{net profit}}{\text{net sales}} = \frac{8.5}{198.4} = 4.3\%$$

Industry standard = 6.8%

In the case of our mythical firm, while the ratios in all the other categories seem to be reasonably close to industry standards, the profitability ratios indicate that this particular firm does indeed vary from industry standards and, therefore, probably has internal management problems. The return on equity was below standard, the return on total assets was below standard, and the profit margin was well below standard. This indicates that the firm's prices are too low or that its costs of operations are too high, or both. In any case, you would check further by asking for additional years of data, by doing a trend analysis of the ratios, and by interviewing the firm's management to determine where the strengths and weaknesses are.

The ratio analysis techniques presented in this section are the tools of the financial community. Corporate controllers and treasurers use them. Financial analysts use them. Your competitors use them. They are important to the corporate real estate executive because

1. They talk the language of the financial community.

2. They provide an understanding of your company, its competitors, and the industry.

3. They help analyze potential partners, tenants, suppliers, contractors, and the like, upon whom your success depends.

4. They help make critical financial decisions in your area of responsibility.

5. They help analyze and guide critical capital investment decisions.

Real Estate Ratio Analysis

Real estate has developed its own ratio analysis techniques. These ratios are normally used to analyze a proposal or pro forma for a new building or the profit-and-loss statement of an existing building. These pro formas and profit-and-loss statements are the "financial statements" of the real estate industry. They contain the same information as the balance sheet and income statement of a corporation.

A proposal for a new real estate project will normally contain a budget, sometimes called a "uses of funds" statement, or a list of various items of investment, including land, construction and equipment, and financing costs, as well as architectural fees and other expenditures necessary to complete the building. Elsewhere in the proposal will be found a section normally titled "sources of funds," indicating how the project will be paid for. The combination of the equity of the proposed owners and the funds to be loaned by the investors will equal the total proposed budget for the project. Thus the uses and sources of funds are in balance.

The pro forma or income statement for the project will be similar to the corporate income statement because it will list the gross revenues. From this income will be subtracted operating expenses for property taxes, repairs and maintenance, contract custodial and grounds services, insurance, management fees, utilities, and supplies. The total operating expenses are subtracted from the gross income to yield the net operating income.

One item that is normally different from the corporate income statement is the treatment of debt service. The corporation normally includes debt service as part of operating expense, but in a real estate project it is given separate treatment. In the corporation all projects are assumed by financial management to be funded from one large capital pool. In the typical real estate investment, however, financial arrangements may be so specialized and designed so specifically for one project that they need to be kept separate. In addition, because of the highly leveraged financing of most real estate transactions, the ability of the project to cover debt service is one of the critical ratios used in analyzing it. Finally, because cash flow is so significant to real estate analysis, the debt service is subtracted from the net operating income after its computation in order to give a picture of the cash flow prior to debt service payment and after. When debt service is subtracted from the net operating income, the net income or cash flow before depreciation is determined. From this figure must be subtracted an estimate of the income taxes due on the project to arrive at a net cash flow, to which depreciation will be added to determine the total cash flow of the project.

The point is that the corporate financial statement and the real estate financial statement are very similar, and, with a little imagination, the ratios which were discussed earlier can be applied to real property statements to gain important insights into the financial condition of a current or proposed project.

Some of these ratios would include the ROI, or *return on investment,* and the ROE, or *return on equity,* which were profitability ratios discussed above. Of a similar nature is the ratio of the sum of the net operating income for the holding period of the investment divided by the number of years to yield the average net operating income per year divided by the total capital invested. This ratio will tell you what to expect on an average basis in the way of return on investment over the life of the project.

$$\frac{\dfrac{\text{Accumulated net income}}{N \text{ years}}}{\text{Total investment}}$$

Other ratios used in analyzing the project would include the *loan value divided by total investment,* which is similar to the long-term debt divided by total assets on the corporate balance sheet, and *equity divided by the total investment* to determine the percentage of ownership in the project.

$$\frac{\text{Loan value}}{\text{Total investment}} \qquad \frac{\text{Equity}}{\text{Total investment}}$$

Two ratios can be used to determine the ability of the project to carry its debt service. First, the *break-even or default ratio,* which is expenses plus debt service divided by gross income, indicates the number of times that the gross income will cover the operating expenses, including debt service.

$$\frac{\text{Operating expenses and debt services}}{\text{Gross income}}$$

The second ratio, *debt service divided by net operating income,* indicates how many times the income of the project after expenses will cover the debt service.

$$\frac{\text{Debt service}}{\text{Net operating income}}$$

These ratios are a measure of risk because the closer this ratio is to 1, the higher the risk that an interruption of the income stream could lead to default on the debt service. Of course, a ratio below 1 indicates that the project cannot carry the debt service as proposed.

The real estate analyst also uses other ratios developed around square-footage costs. These include construction costs, operating costs of various types, and, of course, income per square foot. As with the corporate ratios, all of these real estate ratios are normally compared from one project to the next, from year to year, and measured by various industry standards.

Budgeting Analysis

One final group of calculations that is extremely important in analyzing a real estate project arises from capital budgeting analysis. There are four distinct ratios to look at in accepting or rejecting a capital investment proposal concerning real estate: the payback ratio, the net present value (NPV), the internal rate of return (IRR), and the average rate of return (AVRR).

In order to illustrate each of these, let's assume that our mythical company, XYZ Furniture Manufacturing Company, has before it a proposal to spend $50,000 to install an energy management system. Let's assume further that the company has had three different engineering proposals, which have resulted in the following projections of savings over the first five years of operation.

Table 9.1 shows the projected cash savings estimated by the three engineering studies. A sixth year is included to allow the calculation of a payback ratio based strictly upon the cash flow of the cash savings. The payback ratio is calculated by summing the annual cash flows until the full amount of the original investment is reached. Because the actual date of

Table 9.1. Savings Projection over First Five
Years of Operation

Years	Proposal A	Proposal B	Proposal C
1	7,500	13,200	10,100
2	8,400	11,800	10,100
3	9,400	10,500	10,100
4	10,500	9,400	10,100
5	11,800	8,400	10,100
6	13,200	7,500	10,100

complete return would be between two year-ends, it is a simple matter to interpolate between the two dates to arrive at an estimate of the month in that year in which the payback would be completed. In this manner, the payback periods for the three proposals can be calculated:

Proposal A = 5 years, 2 months

Proposal B = 4 years, 7 months

Proposal C = 4 years, 11 months

To look at the complete picture, depreciation must be added to the savings projected to generate the total cash flow from the projected investment. (For purposes of this analysis, I have eliminated any consideration of the investment tax credit, the energy tax credit, and other tax benefits, which could greatly change this analysis because of the possibility of significant changes in the tax laws in the near future.) Table 9.2 shows the total cash flow for the three proposals, including depreciation of the proposed equipment purchased.

When the payback calculation is based on the total cash flow, including depreciation, Proposal A would pay back in three years one month. The inclusion of the depreciation tends to distort the payback period because it applies depreciation to paying for the asset.

Table 9.2. Total Cash Flow

Years	Proposal A	Proposal B	Proposal C
1	13,750	18,050	16,350
2	14,650	16,750	16,350
3	15,650	16,650	16,350
4	16,750	14,650	16,350
5	18,050	13,750	16,350

Payback Ratio

The *payback ratio* is an excellent measure of how long the funds invested in a project will be at risk. In other words, when the investment is paid back by the cash flow from the project, the original investment is no longer at risk. The ratio is extremely easy to calculate but does have several problems. First, and most important, it does not consider the time value of money. Second, it tends to favor the short term over the long term. Third, it ignores the potential savings and income to be generated by the investment beyond the payback period. If the XYZ Furniture Manufacturing Company uses only the payback method of analysis, it would probably choose Proposal B.

Net Present Value

Because the payback method ignores the time value of money, analysts usually combine it with other techniques to get a better picture of the proposal. The *net present value (NPV)* or *discounted cash flow (DCF)* calculates the amount of money you would need today, invested at a certain rate, to equal a known amount of money at some future date. To illustrate, let's use the cash flow in Proposal C above. This example had an even annual cash flow of $16,350 projected for the first five years of the investment. This would total $81,750 in cash flow at the end of the five-year period. The question is: What amount would have to be invested today, and at what rate, in order to equal the cash flow at the end of the period? The analyst selects a discount rate, or rate at which the investment is assumed to be earning interest. This rate is usually assumed to be the investor's opportunity cost, that is, the highest rate of return which the investor could receive on another investment of equal risk. In the example of the XYZ Company, that rate is assumed to be 12 percent.

A calculator or computer program that calculates net present value can be used. Obviously, this is by far the easiest method to make these rather detailed calculations. The net present values of the cash flows in our example are

Proposal A = +5,982

Proposal B = +7,685

Proposal C = +8,938

If the XYZ Company compared net present values of the three proposals, it would probably choose Proposal C because this indicates that the net worth of their company would be increased by $8,938 over the five-year life of the proposed investment. All three alternatives indicated that they had a return in excess of the assumed 12 percent opportunity cost. The net present value calculation yields a number which, if positive, tells you by how many dollars cash inflows exceed cash outflows when discounted at the given rate. Alternatively, if the number is negative, you know that cash inflows do not equal cash outlays by the calculated amounts.

Internal Rate of Return

The tool which gives you the ability to calculate the rate of return of the accumulated cash flows to the investment, considering the time value of money and the future value of the investment under analysis, is the *internal rate of return*, or *IRR*. This technique calculates the interest rate at which the cash inflows and cash outflows of an investment alternative must be discounted to sum zero or be equal. The IRR calculation is of great value in comparing alternative investments or different financial structures for the same project. This discount rate is the interest rate at which the initial investment would have to be invested in an alternative investment in order to earn the same as the investment under analysis. By far the simplest way to calculate the internal rate of return is to use a calculator or computer program. In our example, the internal rates of return are

Proposal A   16.5%

Proposal B   18.36%

Proposal C   19.0%

The XYZ Company would again choose Proposal C based on the internal rate of return analysis. Proposal B, however, has a very similar internal rate of return.

While the IRR is a most useful tool, it is based on a couple of hidden assumptions which should be mentioned. First, most formulas used for calculating IRR assume that the excess cash flow of the project will be reinvested at the IRR rate. In reality, these funds will not remain in the project but will be reinvested in other investments at other rates. Secondly, in most project analysis the largest single cash flow item in the IRR calculation is the projected sale price of the asset in the last year of the analysis. Be sure that your investment decision is not based on an internal rate of return which is inflated by an unrealistic estimate of future appreciation.

Average Rate of Return

As a final check the analyst may want to do a relatively simple calculation of the *average rate of return*. This compares the average cash flow per year to the initial investment over the holding period of life of the investment to determine what the average return on the investment is calculated to be. The following example from Proposal A above indicates how the calculation is made.

$$\text{AVRR} = \frac{\dfrac{\text{cash flow} - \text{total investment}}{\text{investment life in years}}}{\text{Total investment}} = \frac{\dfrac{78,850 - 50,000}{5}}{50,000}$$

$$= \frac{5,770}{50,000} = 11.54\%$$

The average rate of return on Proposal B is 11.52% and on Proposal C 12.70%.

The cash flow analysis in these examples was intentionally cut off at the fifth year to illustrate two specific dangers in this type of exercise:

1. The failure to look beyond the analysis period at what might occur. In our example, the cash flow trends for Proposal A were ever-increasing. This would be the logical proposal to choose if the cash flows continued to grow at the same percentage rates. On the other hand, Proposal B's cash flows could disappear eventually, while Proposal C's cash flows would remain constant.

2. The failure to recognize that you are analyzing assumptions and estimates, not actual facts. It is important to check the underlying assumptions of the data to be sure that the projections have some basis in reality.

Corporate Finance and Corporate Real Estate

Corporate finance and corporate real estate analysis are synergistic. The major task of corporate financial management is to plan capital expenditures, to help determine whether to increase investments in capital assets, and to finance those investments. The job of the corporate real estate executive is to help create and manage the corporation's fixed assets. The two departments must work hand in glove and should be communicating with each other on a regular basis in a common financial language.

10

Appraisal and Market Analysis

Bernard P. Giroux

Vice President, Marketing, Marathon U.S. Realties, Inc.

H. Dennis Boyle

Vice President, National Sales Director, Appraisal Division
Cushman & Wakefield

The Appraisal

Definition

An *appraisal* is an estimate or opinion of value.[1] A corporate real estate asset manager should seek an opinion of value from an appraiser who has been qualified by at least one of the major appraisal or counseling organizations in the United States. These groups include The American Society of Real Estate Counselors, The American Society of Real Estate Appraisers, The American Society of Appraisers, and The Society of Real Estate

[1] Byrl N. Boyce (ed.), *Real Estate Appraisal Terminology*, Ballinger Publishing Company, Cambridge, MA 1981, p. 14.

139

Appraisers.[2] In addition, the appraiser should have significant experience in evaluating the specific type of property under consideration.

The opinion of value is generally reduced to a formal written report, presented in a format prescribed by current standards of professional appraisal practice. It is important for the corporate real estate manager to understand what the requirements are for an appraisal report, how to read the report, and how to determine from this reading if the appraiser's opinion is supported by the evidence. The report contains information about the property being appraised, the market for it, and the rationale behind the evaluation. Alternative valuations should be presented by the appraiser if the property warrants it.

The appraiser should provide a report that enables the client to make a decision about real property. The value of the appraiser lies in an ability to determine from the evidence available the value of a property. Although the appraiser estimates market value, the appraiser and the corporate client determine in advance what form of value is sought.[3] The corporate real estate manager must have the ability to interpret the information presented by the appraiser and introduce it into the proper framework for management decisions. The appraisal, therefore, should be read completely. It is primarily a valuation report, but the information it contains may communicate other facts useful in the corporate decision-making process.

Appraisal Applications

The appraisal is traditionally used to establish the value of a property for transfer of ownership. It may also be used to set the limits of value for lending purposes or in eminent domain proceedings. There are instances where properties are appraised on a continuing basis to determine unrealized asset value, that is, the difference between book value and market value.

Because appraisals are used in the corporate decision-making process, the appraiser is obligated to inform the client fully about research results. The appraiser also has an obligation to state what market factors are at work that will directly affect the immediate market value and potential future value of the property. Corporate real estate executives should be managing real property assets for results. Appraisals are an integral part of any capital asset review process.

[2] Maury Seldin and Lynn N. Woodward (eds.), *The Real Estate Handbook*, Dow Jones-Irwin, Homewood, IL, 1980, p. 112.

[3] Richard U. Ratcliff, *Valuation for Real Estate Decisions*, Democrat Press, Santa Cruz, CA, 1972, p. 1.

Limitations of the Report

An appraisal report is limited by the focus of the appraiser and the requirements placed upon the appraiser by the corporate client. It is also limited by the definition of value. Value is determined as of a specific date, and considerable historic evidence is used for establishing value. Although weight is given to future cash flows, an appraisal is not a feasibility analysis, nor does it usually consider the specific investment criteria of a buyer or the corporate client. Appraisals, therefore, should be judged only by how well they describe a property and how accurately they establish value at a particular point in the present or for whatever time is specified.

Selection of an Appraiser

Background and Experience—Its Relevance

An appraiser who has spent a career appraising single-family homes may, in theory, be qualified to appraise a regional shopping center, a large apartment complex, or an office facility, but, in practice, the appraiser does not have the sense of the marketplace or the experience necessary for the analysis required in complex reports. An appraiser not qualified to perform a particular assignment should admit it and refer the assignment to a qualified professional. Some appraisers may undertake an assignment falsely claiming relevant experience and can cause a serious loss to the client. One appraiser, for example, claimed to have had experience testifying at hearings for planning and zoning matters. After producing an excellent study on the impact of the location of a regional mall near a residential area, the appraiser did not properly present the case before a zoning board, costing a developer the zoning permits. As it turned out, that hearing had been the appraiser's first!

Corporate managers should qualify appraisers, making sure to know who the best ones are for the type of property under consideration. Certain appraisers are experts in determining the value of recycled or rehabilitated property. Others may specialize in the evaluation of shopping centers or office buildings. Having a designation may indicate some level of training, but it does not guarantee experience. Appraisers should show the corporate client sufficient examples of their work that demonstrate their capability.

The best appraisers may not always be local, although they may have a comprehensive understanding of local market conditions. The facility being appraised may be of such a size and value that the market for the facility is regional or national in character. Local appraisers may not have access to data that firms with regional or national experience do. Thus a key criterion for an appraiser to meet should be experience with the type of property under consideration.

Staff Support—A Necessary Ingredient

Appraising is a business with many entrepreneurs. They operate alone or in small organizations, maintaining as little overhead as possible. This limits their capacity for assignments and also normally narrows their exposure to various problems, consequently limiting their breadth of experience. National firms, such as Cushman & Wakefield, Landauer and Associates, and Real Estate Research, to name a few, have the large and experienced staffs required to perform large-scale, multiple-property analyses. They also have staff experienced in solving complex special problems, as well as the data banks necessary to determine if a regional or national market exists for properties. The larger the scope of the assignment, the more it taxes the resources of the small appraisal shop. A single appraiser, evaluating a 1 million-square-foot warehouse, will give up many smaller assignments in order to complete the report for the corporate client. It may reduce fees somewhat, but it is more important to the corporate client to have reliable documentation, research, and presentation.

The Requirement for Objectivity

In all appraisals objectivity is essential. Discussion of numbers to be "achieved" in a report is just not ethical.[4] The appraiser should be able to provide the client with more information than the client imagined, allowing conclusions to be drawn from independent reading and analysis of what the appraiser has said. Because the appraiser may have to testify about the validity of the report, it must be based on an objective and impartial analysis of the facts presented. The corporate manager should realize that there is significant benefit to this objectivity. With an outside appraisal based on research that is not influenced by corporate thinking, the conclusions presented to senior management are more readily accepted.

---

[4] American Institute of Real Estate Appraisers, *Professional Ethics and Standards,* Chicago, 1985, Canon 3, pp. 7–11.

Communications with a Corporate Staff

Management's Objectives

The corporate client should be clear about what management's objectives are before ordering an appraisal and must convey these objectives to the appraiser. The appraiser must then define what the objective of the particular report should be. Confusion about objectives is difficult to deal with. An appraiser may be three-quarters through a report and get a shift in objectives owing to a lack of prior communication by the corporate client. This leads to delays, greater expense, and conflicts. Corporations, therefore, should keep their appraisal objectives simple and clear-cut. If a retail company, for example, holds a leasehold interest in a store, management should expect from the appraiser a realistic summary of its value based on the duration of the lease, a thorough analysis of current economic rent, the impact of operating covenants or other obligations that encumber the leasehold, and alternative uses based upon an analysis of other retail and commercial activity affecting the site.

Management Decision Support

The information contained in the appraisal's narrative section should be summarized in one or two pages at the beginning of the report. Management decisions about real property are generally made by senior executives and, depending upon the magnitude of the proposal, may reach the board of directors. An appraiser should be able to defend the report, to answer questions asked by senior managers both familiar and unfamiliar with real estate. The corporate real estate manager, therefore, has a two-way communication function because the information in the appraisal should tell senior management what it needs to know to acquire, sell, lease, appeal a tax or eminent domain decision, or address other problems of the property under study. The corporate real estate manager is the conduit through which the appraiser and senior management exchange questions and answers.

Corporate Measure of Value

The Reason for an Appraisal

Corporate real property always has value, but corporate real estate assets may not be thought to have value, other than book value, until their use as operational facilities has ended. They then become potential sources of cash to help maintain corporate liquidity. An appraiser, therefore, is often called upon to evaluate a corporate facility when the question arises, "Can this asset generate any cash?" Corporations may require appraisals at other times for the following reasons:

Acquisition and development.   Whether acquisition takes the form of a purchase, lease, or other form of addition to the asset base, an appraisal is required. A corporation may acquire and rehabilitate older space; it may acquire land to construct additional facilities. In such cases, an appraiser should determine a basic value indicating the impact of acquisition or development.

Sale.   The sale of corporate property usually requires senior management approval. Management requires justification and support for its decision, which an appraisal provides. The current and future market for a particular property should be known prior to deciding on a sale. Residuals may be available to the corporation in the form of subleases, leases, or other operating arrangements, which may be more financially desirable than a sale.

Financing.   Real estate can be used to finance a corporation's cash needs. It may be financed through a third party. Appraisals are critical to financing. The value of a financed facility should clearly support the size of the loan.

Redevelopment.   Corporations recycle older properties or readapt them. An appraisal may examine the viability of this reuse or redevelopment and determine the value of alternative uses for the facility. This will enable the corporation to decide whether it will allow for participation in residuals, execute a joint venture to effect the redevelopment, or sell to a developer for completion of the redevelopment.

Equity questions.   Where there is an issue of fairness, the appraiser may render an opinion of value which supports an appeal for correction of an injustice. Excess tax payments, for example, directly affect bottom-line results. Properties that are overassessed and unfairly taxed require expert evaluation to contest the assessments. Appraisers also serve as expert witnesses in land damage cases or eminent domain proceedings. They may also be called upon to evaluate properties in foreclosure or in merger and acquisition activities.

Corporate Properties—Peculiarities

The common peculiarity of a corporate property is that it generally produces no income. Although corporations occupy space and may charge an internal "rent" for use of capital tied up in facilities, this is not income generated from an outside source but an internal accounting technique used to gauge the productivity or efficiency of the unit occupying the space.

Another aberration exists in the custom-built facility. A chemical company, for example, may build a plant suitable for producing resins or paints. The opinion of value of this facility has to be tempered by a realistic appraisal of the business itself and a comprehensive look at the industry to determine if there is a market for it. The facility may have value in use, but the market for such a surplus facility may not exist. More practically, a multistory distribution facility may be available for sale. The question would then be one of location and adaptable reuse. Several large distribution facilities have been recently adapted to office and retail use. Location and market demand drive the decision for this type of reuse.

In certain instances a modern industrial facility may suffer from obsolescence. Large-scale buildings of simple construction may have excessive capacity that is not readily marketable. Demand for a facility type may be regional, but a facility may be located in the wrong county or state. In other instances, corporations tack on ancillary facilities, such as offices, computer centers, or truck depots, which are not readily useful to other potential occupants. Retail facilities also suffer from owner-induced obsolescence because of shape, number of floors, attached warehouses, and other features. They also are encumbered by reciprocal easement and operating agreements (REAs) which tie the operation of the facility to a term of years. Retail facilities are joined in shopping malls by a common business purpose which is linked legally by the REA. Anchor tenants must agree to operate and pay rent and other associated costs in order to maintain customer acceptance and traffic, control market share, and maintain the anchor-store to satellite-tenant relationship which exists in all shopping centers.

The peculiarity of corporate properties makes them hard to manage as assets. Operating costs are buried within operating statements that do not contain line items for real estate expenses. The appraiser must take into account what these costs are. For example, real estate, personal property, and other taxes are sometimes lumped together in a one-line item. Unless the corporate real estate manager has a good system of monitoring them, the determination of real property operating costs can be frustrated by long examinations of accounting records. Few companies operate their real property from a central, computer-based data management system; consequently, the corporate manager must explain the data or provide them to the appraiser directly. The appraiser must, therefore, identify those peculiarities of a corporate property which will affect the valuation problem. These issues are numerous, and the nature of corporate property makes each appraisal different from the last. The factors creating these differences should be familiar to the appraiser and drive the evaluation of each property.

Valuation versus Investment Analysis

An appraisal or valuation analysis is generally considered an opinion of current fair market value. Fair market value may be determined by several standard methods: cost approach, market data approach, and income approach. The value of corporate real estate, however, should be measured by its capacity to produce some form of return for the capital invested. Ownership of corporate real estate means that (a) corporate funds are directly invested in the property, (b) the corporation has used borrowed funds in some sort of financial leaseback transaction, (c) the property is mortgaged, usually on the basis of the strength of the corporation's financial statement, or (d) the property is leased by the corporation, tying up someone else's capital. The appraiser must, therefore, deal with the value to the corporation under conditions of continued occupancy and use of the facility or for disposition in any of its various forms. In determining the most probable value, the analysis is generally driven by market-derived factors. These measure the productivity of the corporate capital invested in real estate by indicating whether in competing for investment funds the real estate investment is producing a return equal to, or better than, the market rate.

Investment analysis is generally deemed to be an analysis of a property on the basis of the requirements of a specific investor over the planned period of ownership, subject to certain tax requirements. The discounted cash flow method (DCF) is generally used to evaluate property for investment. This form of analysis may be applied to corporate property by using corporate-driven criteria to determine market value or investment value based on assumptions derived from corporate financial planning criteria.

The corporate manager, therefore, needs to analyze how the appraiser will approach the valuation question. Guidelines should be given the appraiser on what the corporate hurdle rates and the corporate guidelines and assumptions are for invested capital. The appraiser should be aware of what alternative investment opportunities are competing for the capital invested in real estate as well as how market-derived or internal forces will affect the demand for that capital.

The Appraisal Report

The Report in a Corporate Environment

Appraisal reports have various functions in a corporate environment, but they are always used for decision making. Here we discuss how to review a report and determine if the report meets stated objectives.

The Purpose of the Report

In examining the purpose of a report, the corporate manager and the appraiser must agree on which value is being sought. If a report is being prepared to determine the value for financing a facility through a sale-leaseback, then the tax position of the proposed investors will serve as a determinant of investment value. If a report is prepared for the disposition of a department store, then market-derived factors will figure most importantly in the report. There should be a clear distinction between what type of value is sought: *market value* or *investment value.*

A third type of value may exist for the corporate manager: *value in use,* derived by determining the productivity of a facility. No value may exist for a facility except the value created by its use. Without that use, there would be no market-derived value.

A fourth type of value is the *value in exchange,* which follows from tax-free swaps and other forms of trading of financial or economic interests.

In condemnation proceedings, the appraiser calculates the *value of damages* caused by a taking. An appraiser will determine the fair market value of a property before a taking. The effect of the action on the property is then examined and an estimate is made of the fair market value after the taking. The difference between the two figures is the value of damages which would be sought in an eminent domain case.

The appraiser and corporate manager must also clarify what rights are to be appraised. Property may be owned in fee with no debt; it may be held as a leasehold; the interest valued may be partial; there may be value in addition to leasehold value; a leasehold advantage may exist. The appraiser must also consider whether the valuation is for a cash transaction or cash equivalents. There may be other terms involved, which the corporate manager should disclose to the appraiser.

The Scope of the Report

An appraisal report should follow an outline prescribed by the current standards of professional practice. If the report is in an abbreviated letter format, rather than a longer narrative, the data supporting the opinion of value should be available for review. The assumptions according to which a report has been drafted should limit its scope. The report should determine what factors in the available data most affect the property. The appraiser has an obligation to narrow the focus of the report to four specific issues: the economics of the property, its financial characteristics, the market for it, and the impact of the socioeconomic environment in which the property sits.

Each section of the appraiser's report should relate to the central purpose of the report, focusing on the relevant data which will narrow the scope of the report to a manageable set of issues, alternatives, and justifiable conclusions.

Physical Property Data

The corporate manager has a responsibility to supply the appraiser with as much information about the physical characteristics of a property as possible. Without it, the appraiser must rely on third-party sources, which are not always accurate. Information that should be given to the appraiser includes surveys, plot plans, legal descriptions, title reports, aerial photographs, copies of deeds, construction specifications, and equipment specifications.

Detailed property descriptions should provide type of construction; age; gross dimensions; square footage; ceiling heights; column spacing; the number and location of loading doors; docks, ramps, and other service areas; details on sprinkler and mechanical systems; floor loadings; roof construction; railcar capacities; parking areas; fencing; lighting; retention ponds or surface drainage requirements; ratios of land to building area; ratios of office area to building area; and the net to gross efficiency ratios. The corporate client should have these data readily available.

Ownership

Surveys should have legal descriptions attached. As-built surveys should be performed on new buildings and updates done on older structures. Deeds and title reports should be available, sale-leaseback or other types of credit-financing documents should be given to the appraiser. The appraiser must also have the latest title changes, including easement information and other recent encumbrances.

Ownership data give the appraiser a clear picture of the rights being appraised. The form of ownership must be clear. Property may be owned by entities other than the client's company. If subsidiaries are involved, the appraiser must know this.

Mortgage Data

Many corporate properties are mortgaged. Some are held by subsidiary entities so that the parent corporation does not exercise direct control. The appraiser may ignore a mortgage and value in fee simple, or the leverage effect of a mortgagee may be taken into account. If a mortgagee has an interest in the facility, documentation should be provided to the appraiser.

Leasehold Data

The appraisal of leasehold property is most complex. Basic lease documents, all subsequent amendments, letter agreements, that is, all terms and conditions of the lease which affect the present financial performance of the property, should be reviewed. Executory costs, including basic rentals, percentage clauses, and operating covenants, have a significant effect on value.

Retail leases tied to reciprocal construction, operating, and easement agreements (RCOEs) need to be thoroughly examined by the appraiser. RCOE documents are usually voluminous and difficult to read, but their effect is staggering. Operating covenants are generally required by lenders and small tenants to hold the anchor stores in major malls. Major retailers cannot ignore these covenants because they call for severe penalties in the event of termination by an anchor tenant. Operating covenants are most damaging to leasehold interests because they may force a tenant to remain in an unprofitable situation.

If the corporate client has a lease abstract, it should be given to the appraiser. Once an appraiser has read and summarized a lease, the summary should be reviewed by the client and the client's lawyer for accuracy.

It is important that the future impact of a lease be considered. For example, percentage rent payments without adjustments for taxes, common-area-maintenance payments, or other executory costs become very expensive during periods of rapid inflation. The payment of percentage rent, in addition to minimum rents, may turn a profitable facility into a loser.

The client may or may not have flexibility under a lease agreement. The right to assign or sublet the lease is important in a disposition problem. The use clause of a lease may limit the types of operators to which one may assign or sublease. Leases present opportunities to generate profits from subleases or assignments. This is unrealized potential in ongoing leasehold situations, but the corporate manager should be apprised that the potential does exist, given a proper appraisal. As an example, if a 70,000-square-foot retail facility is leased on a long-term basis with 15 years remaining on the base term of a lease executed 10 years ago, there is a potential rental advantage because of the age of the lease. The base rent 10 years ago may have been $2.25 to $2.50 per square foot on a net basis. Today, that same facility, if it is in good physical condition and in a location which has not become economically obsolete, may command a rent of $3.50 to $3.75 per square foot. On the basis of a calculation of the present worth of the rental advantage ($3.75 − $2.50 = $1.25), discounted at 12 percent for 15 years, there is a potential leasehold interest of about $600,000 or an annual subrental profit of $87,500. If there were options beyond 15 years, the property would have even more value. The various lease clauses which impact on this potential have to be taken into account by the appraiser. The pure economic judgment of value must be tempered by consideration of the assignment and sublet clauses, percentage clauses, operating covenants, and other obligations which may encumber the corporate manager's ability to profit from a leasehold interest.

Other Financial Data

The appraiser should seek whatever financial data exist on corporate property. Sale-leaseback information is complex and not easily analyzed. Buy-back provisions and other controls affect a corporation's ability to use its assets.

Corporate subsidiaries may also control real property. These subsidiaries may be organized in such a manner that determination of value is difficult because debt may be placed on these properties on the basis of a corporation's credit worthiness, not the individual property's ability to produce income.

Comparable Corporate Property

Corporations have records of their properties which have been previously sold, financed, or leased and the conditions under which these transactions occurred. The appraiser should evaluate these data.

Highest and Best Use

This is one of the most important sections of the appraisal report. It ties together the various analyses produced by the appraiser and supports the approach the appraiser will take in the mathematical estimation of value. It should provide the basis for analysis of alternatives to the standard answers given in reports. Its logic should be defensible, and the conclusion should be based not only on evidence of fact but also on the appraiser's experience. The corporate manager should judge the quality of an appraiser's report by the manner in which highest and best use is developed and should challenge assumptions or conditions presented by the appraiser.

Methodology—Tradition and Variation

The cost, market-data, and income approaches are traditional methods used in estimating real property values. The corporate manager should concentrate on a review of the rationale which the appraiser uses in each approach.

The cost approach analyzes the current costs of developing and constructing property similar to the subject. Once a cost estimate is produced, using standard sources of current construction costs, a detailed analysis of functional, physical, and economic obsolescence is made; this is applied as a reduction to the construction cost, and a value estimate is produced. The cost approach is usually not an effective gauge of value and is often ignored or excluded from reports by appraisers.

In the market-data approach, the appraiser examines sales or leases or properties with characteristics similar to the subject. The most probable selling price or fair market value is then determined from the conditions of sale or lease of the comparable properties with evaluations of financial, physical, and economic data generated from the market. No opinion of value using this method is complete without a realistic assessment of comparable information or the current and projected market situation where the subject property is located.

The market-data or comparable-transactions approach should be carefully scrutinized. In determining land value, does the appraiser use comparable parcels in size, location, zoning, and time of sale? Are speculative trends accounted for? Are similar properties used in the analysis? Has the appraiser taken into account whether the market for a property is regional, national, or local? What trends in the market, as depicted in the background data of the report, has the appraiser used to justify estimates of value? Is the analysis of the market itself sufficient? Are all the factors of supply and demand taken into account?

The income approach requires a comprehensive understanding of the application of financial analysis to real estate. It also demands the ability to interpret and apply market-derived financial data to the analysis of real property. A facility is assumed to have a specified useful life, or it may produce income in a manner limited by the terms and conditions of a lease. Assumptions, based on analysis of the market-derived financial data, are made about the quality, quantity, and timing of the income which the property is assumed or imputed to produce. The income stream is then capitalized, using an appropriate method, and an indication of value is derived.

In the income approach, it is important that the appraiser make a correct judgment about how the market perceives the property under study. Is a property normally bought by projecting and discounting the future value of cash flows? Or is the property generally bought and sold using a gross income multiplier? Should the appraiser use some form of discounted cash flow (DCF) analysis? Has the impact of financing been accounted for? Are alternative methods of analysis under this approach discussed? If the DCF methods are applied, what specific assumptions did the appraiser use in the model and are they realistic? Income property analysis is interest-rate-sensitive. The appraiser has to know how income properties are bought and sold locally, regionally, and nationally to offer a sound judgment.

The corporate real estate executive has the responsibility for determining if these traditional methods have been utilized in their proper context and if variations on the theme should be employed to assist the appraiser.

Conclusion

Report Summation

The appraisal report should be summarized concisely and must clearly state the opinion of value, which should accurately represent what the corporate manager can expect from the marketplace. The exhibits and addenda to the report should support the analysis. The report should accurately portray the site, the facility, the construction, the comparables, and their location. Letter appraisals should indicate that support data are available, and the corporate manager should check this fact occasionally. The corporate real estate executive should also be fully aware of the current standards of professional practice of each appraisal society and judge reports accordingly. The appraiser should be willing to provide the corporate manager with information about standards. The more knowledgeable and demanding the client, the better the appraisal is likely to be.

11

Corporate Real Estate Negotiations— A Discipline, Not an Art Form

William J. Scarpino

Vice President, Collins Foods International, Inc.

John Wayne in the Orient

Negotiators from the Orient find the typical American negotiator ailing from the John Wayne syndrome. Americans typically enter negotiating situations with their hands poised near the butts of six-shooters (they always wear two!), eyes darting from side to side, looking for the black hats. When the smoke clears, they check their wounds, count their losses, and calculate who won. Sad, but true. Americans show little finesse in their negotiating style, technique, and strategy. By being the biggest and the strongest, they expect to win because that's how Hopalong Cassidy, the Lone Ranger, and Matt Dillon won.

This American style is more understandable when you realize what a young country America is compared to those of the Orient. The older cultures have learned over time the fundamentals of *subtle* negotiating and apply them when dealing with the American John Waynes.

Typically "John" arrives in Japan, let us say, to negotiate a substantial contract. He has a week booked at a good hotel and a return flight Sunday at noon. He expects to get down to business first thing Monday morning and wrap up business by Thursday, leaving Friday and Saturday to see the sights.

He is slightly puzzled when he is greeted by his business counterparts on Monday and taken on a tour of the city rather than going to the negotiating table. That evening the *sake* flows and John finds the Oriental hospitality charming. Three days and three more tours of the countryside later, complete with evening entertainment, including lots of *sake*, our negotiator is getting a bit rough around the edges. He knows that he should get down to business, but whenever he mentions it to his hosts, they suggest another sight he simply must see and tell him there's plenty of time to work out the contract because "we're really not so far apart."

Finally, late Saturday afternoon the business meeting is set for the next morning, just before John's flight at noon. "Well," rationalizes our American hero, "they are as tired as I am, and they have been great hosts. There's really no reason we can't work things out quickly, especially after the rapport we've developed over this last week."

Morning arrives, and as the American walks into the conference room, he is surprised when his hosts excuse themselves and are replaced by a fresh negotiating team. Four hours later our red-eyed, *sake*-dulled, fallen hero boards his plane in defeat.

A tall story? Not if you talk with experienced international negotiators. They know the other side's strategy and either take steps to control it or pace themselves to offset its impact.

The Process of Negotiation

The process of negotiation involves the interaction of people. The John Wayne style of negotiating assumes that there is not enough money or product to go around, that people are basically greedy, and that you need to outsmart the next person to win. By contrast, the experienced negotiator knows that there is usually a large enough pie to be shared equitably, that most people are not driven by irrational greed, and that for an agreement to survive the test of time, both parties must be content (though not always happy) with its terms.

Negotiation is the process of creating a mutual understanding between the parties about the relative merits of their respective positions. To achieve this environment of understanding there are four basic principles that need to be followed. First, take the time to create a comfortable negotiating environment, one in which neither side is threatened. Second, separate problems from conflicts so that the problems can be creatively analyzed and evaluated. Third, identify and understand each other's needs. Fourth, structure the agreement in a fashion to meet as many of the identified needs as possible. Agreements negotiated by this approach are much more likely to survive the ensuing period of documentation than a John Wayne "blow 'em away" transaction, where each side tabulates its losses rather than its benefits.

Negotiating Maturity

To apply these basic negotiating principles effectively, we need to appreciate that people are different and that they react according to their maturity level. It's not how well educated, how affluent, or even how powerful a person is, but how mature the person is that is important during negotiations. The process of maturation evolves through five distinct stages.

Stage 1: The Controller.   This is the infant stage. The controller uses demands and threats to prevail. The controller does not see contradictions, is locked into a rigid position, and cannot or will not try to understand the other side. The controller is quite immature and threatened, regardless of wealth, position, or power.

Stage 2: The Tabulator.   This is the preadolescent stage, where scoring points is all-important. Tabulators know that others have feelings and thoughts, but feel they will be outsmarted and taken advantage of if they let their own feelings show. They assume that all the others are out to line their pockets as much as possible. This is the most common stage in the American business world. Tabulators are literal, direct, aggressive, and suspicious of others.

Stage 3: The Facilitator.   This is the adolescent stage, marked by the onset of abstract thinking. The facilitator understands the feelings and needs of others, especially the need for approval, and will do anything to make a problem disappear, that is, anything to avoid confrontation. In negotiations, facilitators are likely to give everything away to make a deal, if making the deal will gain them praise from their peers and superiors.

Stage 4: The Producer.   This is the adult stage. Having grown tired of giving everything away to gain the respect of others, producers focus their efforts on projects they believe in. Their thinking becomes polarized, dichotomous, and egocentric. They are effective because they believe in themselves and their projects. They are tough, independent, and very productive. They think in alternatives and extract opportunities from problems. They know their objectives and work diligently to make things happen to attain success.

Stage 5: The Actualizer.   This is the benefactor stage. Powerful, effective, and productive, actualizers are confident enough to trust their ability to analyze and solve problems for the good of all in terms of multiple possibilities. They coach and nurture others to work out the best of many solutions to a problem. They employ team concepts and encourage a harmonious solution to problems obstructing agreement.

Many negotiators have matured to the facilitator stage, but when placed in a stressful or threatening environment, they often revert to the less mature tabulator or controller stage. It is important to understand this and control the negotiating environment and the impact a threatening atmosphere has on the negotiator under stress.

Experience versus Effectiveness

Everyone is an experienced negotiator, but there are few truly effective negotiators. Unless we take the time to develop our skills, techniques, and strategies, we will remain at best only partially effective.

Negotiating is a lifelong experience. From our first cry for food, we are negotiating: peace and quiet for nourishment. Later on we offer good behavior for the right to use the family car, pledges of love for a kiss, corporate loyalty and hard work for a steady paycheck and the opportunity to climb the corporate ladder. We are constantly bartering in life, and we bring innate skills to the negotiating table—raw skills, to say the least.

Companies Are Experienced, Too

The trained corporate negotiator brings more than innate skills to negotiations. Within the corporate environment a negotiator has the potential to develop unique abilities, techniques, and disciplines. A company's broad base of activities and the large number of transactions in its corporate archives can provide an excellent resource library. Through association with the company, the corporate negotiator has the indirect expertise of more transactions than most independent negotiators ever dream of making. It is this corporate knowledge that gives the company representative the ability to perceive alternative solutions to problems and, consequently, to receive concessions that others would not even think of seeking.

The negotiating strength of any corporation lies in the resources it brings to bear against a given opportunity. Of a company's resources, the most important are its people. The corporate negotiator should be trained to orchestrate the resources available from the legal, accounting, finance, tax, engineering, and operating departments. No matter what the issue, there are usually qualified consultants to call upon from within the company's ranks to help solve any problems.

When entering the negotiating arena, the corporate negotiator represents a large and diversified team. The corporate team rarely enters the negotiating session en masse. Rather, the team serves as a resource to the negotiator during the research and planning phases of the actual negotiations.

An effective negotiator is made, not born. The inexperienced corporate negotiator is provided with an arsenal of company facts, corporate policies, and procedures with which to negotiate for the company. In some cases, the new negotiator is afforded training about the company, its operating concepts, real estate policies, and general objectives before being placed in the field. If the corporate environment provides the negotiator a regimen of order, discipline, training, and the support of a corporate team, the negotiator can rapidly become a strong and formidable representative, serving the company well.

Most companies, however, rush their negotiators through an abbreviated training program and then place them in the field to learn while on the job. These novice corporate negotiators are often managed by people outside the real estate group, whose proclivity is to make deals at almost any price to nurture the company's growth plan. This is a haphazard approach to corporate real estate negotiations, and the bones of many companies that followed this practice are scattered across Wall Street. Corporate real estate negotiations, while often positioned low on the corporate priority ladder, have significant impact on the fiscal well-being of any rapidly expanding company.

Beyond "Win/Win" Need Theory: A Corporate Perspective

Many who have studied negotiations are aware of Maslow's hierarchy of needs and its importance for negotiations. Maslow refined Herzberg's original theory of need. Maslow states that people react in any situation on the basis of their current status in life. People first strive to survive, to have adequate water and food. Then they seek to provide creature comforts: clothing and shelter. Next they seek more esoteric rewards: more material possessions and the respect of others. Finally, they seek self-actualization: contributing to society in an attempt to achieve immortality. People will fight for each of these different needs in a different manner. The more basic the need, the more brutal the struggle.

We must understand Maslow's basic need theory as it applies to corporate real estate negotiations. First, we must equate the four levels of need to a real estate deal, in this case to the needs of a developer.

Basic survival	=	Making debt service payments.
Creature comforts	=	Achieving the projected after-tax return.
Esoteric rewards	=	Being 100 percent preleased and enjoying the praise of one's peers and the financial community.
Self-actualization	=	Having the project considered to be an art form in the community and a standard by which future projects are measured.

Now let us evaluate how this developer will react to a below-market rent offer from an excellent potential tenant.

Scenario 1. If the developer is very large, well funded, and ahead of the leasing program, the developer will probably be concerned about architectural design issues and minor lease clauses. The negotiating environment will be elevated to a professional and mature level with ample exchange of information and creative problem solving to satisfy the needs of the negotiators.

Scenario 2. If the developer is moderately large, the project is built and 70 percent occupied, and basic debt service is covered, the developer should be concerned about tenant mix, overage rent, rent escalation, and use of the premises. The negotiating environment will probably be comfortable but firm, affording the opportunity for a fair amount of give-and-take deal making.

Scenario 3. If the developer is small, overextended, and underleased and has cash flow problems, the developer will give almost anything to get an adequate basic rent but will fight to the death when you try to go below the debt service mark and will become defensively abusive if you get too close to the "real" bottom line.

Corporations have added another dimension to the standard need-theory concept. The corporate negotiator has a double set of needs to consider when negotiating. A corporation is a legal being, having unique goals, objectives, and needs. Thus the corporate negotiator has not only personal needs but those of the company to consider in each transaction. The corporate negotiator must identify, evaluate, and satisfy the needs of both the negotiating counterparts and the company.

Thus, in a basic lease transaction the need hierarchy looks like Figure 11-1. The lessee must know the company's goals and objectives, his or her performance goals and objectives, the lessor's company's goals and objectives, and the lessor's own goals and objectives *and* must define the issue *before* starting to work on a solution to the problem. This is difficult enough to accomplish, and, unfortunately, there is more to consider.

Most people shroud their real needs by creating a second dimension of needs to be dealt with, as Figure 11-2 illustrates. Brokers, if they had their way, would act as a buffer between the principals. If they are allowed to do this, the situation becomes hopelessly complex, as shown in Figure 11-3. How can two corporate agents negotiate with so many filters and barriers between them?

The first rule of effective negotiating, therefore, is to deal face to face and principal to principal whenever possible. Only then do you have a chance of identifying each other's actual needs and structuring the deal to satisfy as many of them as possible.

Without discovering the other negotiator's needs, you are simply auctioning an item. You will have only money to deal with and cannot possibly structure a transaction in the best interests of your company. By identifying the other party's needs, the more experienced negotiator is able to structure acceptable trade-offs that allow both sides to win, save face, and live with the agreement. In this way, negotiators move beyond their tradi-

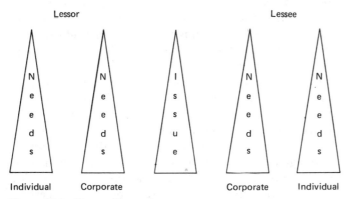

Figure 11.1. The need hierarchy.

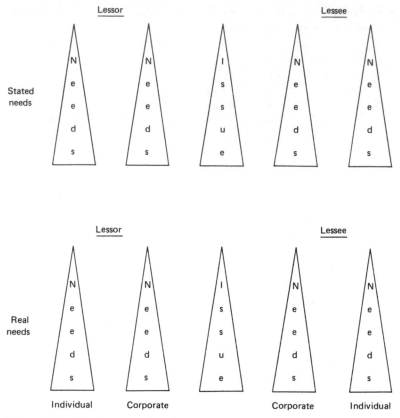

Figure 11.2. Stated versus real needs.

tional adversarial roles and become actualizers, working together and evaluating all available alternatives, then reaching agreement in such a way that both sides can measure the positive reasons for consummating the transaction rather than regretting what they were forced to leave on the negotiating table.

Corporate standards can assist this process. Before entering any transaction, a prudent negotiator will establish goals and objectives. For the corporate negotiator, the company's goals and objectives must be fully understood, too. These corporate goals and objectives must be provided by management. Each company has certain criteria that it considers acceptable, and it is obligated to provide a clear and concise statement of these standards to the negotiator in the field. Learning, understanding, and appreciating the company's specific needs are essential to success.

The Consummate Corporate Negotiator

What distinguishes an effective corporate negotiator? As noted before, everyone has been negotiating from the moment of birth. We are all practiced negotiators. Even the most natural negotiators, however, need to refine their skills to become consistently effective.

The corporate negotiator must be a skilled manager of the tools of the trade, an able communicator, practiced researcher, skilled organizer, and eloquent speaker. Effective negotiators need to be able to assess each situation and secure optimal results by using planned negotiating strategies and tactics. Once goals and objectives are clearly defined, the effective

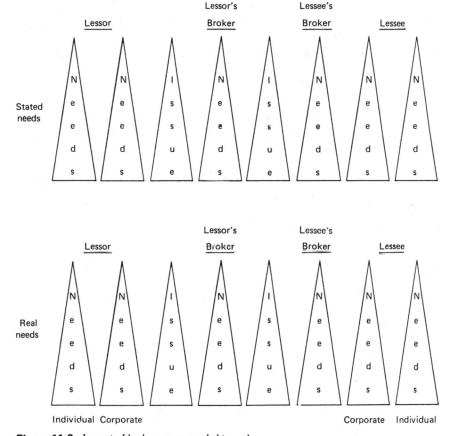

Figure 11.3. Impact of brokerage on needs hierarchy.

negotiator uses an established framework of strategies and tactics to achieve them.

Furthermore, the corporate negotiator, who typically works independently, must have an inner drive to excel. Only the negotiator knows if the plan necessary to secure the best possible deal has been properly prepared and executed. It takes a special dedication to place company needs ahead of a personal need to make deals, to look good in the short term at the long-term expense of the firm. Since they are typically underpaid in comparison with counterparts in commercial real estate, corporate negotiators are faced with abundant opportunities to be led astray. They therefore must recognize and value the rewards and benefits of being part of a corporate structure. Integrity is essential.

Any corporate negotiator who fully understands the company's needs, objectives, and policies has the opportunity to negotiate successfully against even the most experienced opponent. By doing the necessary homework and knowing the facts about a transaction, the corporate negotiator can compete effectively with the veteran deal maker to reach mutually acceptable terms, provided both parties want to make the deal.

The Cycle of Negotiations

Negotiating is a three-part activity comprising preparation, interaction, and follow-up. Preparation, or foreplay, is the prenegotiation, fact-finding period. Interaction is the actual negotiating session, where the parties meet face to face and attempt to work out the deal. Follow-up, or afterplay, is the depressurization period after interaction. Any given transaction is likely to embody several of these negotiation cycles, and the afterplay phase connects each cycle with the next.

Before any negotiating confrontation, the parties must study the property, comparable properties, competition for the property, and each other. The parties may talk with each other informally about the weather, their personal concerns, sports, brokers, anything that comes to mind. What is really taking place is the exchange of personal data. The parties are researching one another. This is a necessary prerequisite to a good negotiation and is an important part of the foreplay phase. During this phase, the negotiators are updating and revising preplanned strategies based on the newly gathered input. During the actual negotiation, the interaction phase, the parties test their tactics and strategies. Problems are isolated and identified, compromises are agreed upon, needs are satisfied, and, with luck, hard work, and perseverance, progress is made.

The contest over, the negotiation enters the afterplay stage, perhaps the most important because the parties disengage, count their gains and losses, relax, and rebuild their personal bonds in preparation for the next cycle of negotiations. The parties can now reinforce each other, compliment each other's negotiating skills, and make a personal commitment to move forward together toward ultimate consummation of the transaction.

Dare to Ask!

To be an effective negotiator one must possess the self-confidence to seek concessions that are seemingly unobtainable. Like students in a classroom who are reluctant to raise their hands, so, too, most people are reluctant to ask for something that might elicit ridicule. Only by asking, however, will a negotiator know if a concession can be granted. The key to this approach is being able to back up your request with a logical reason why it should be granted.

One company's negotiations on the lease of a prime site in California illustrates this point. The prospective tenant had done an excellent job of verifying comparable rental rates to be $2.50 to $2.75 per square foot. The landlord was asking $2.75. The site was undoubtedly one of the best West Coast locations for the tenant. The competition in the area was fierce, and the site would not be on the market for long. The tenant's negotiator, just before meeting with the landlord, told the broker that he was going to offer $2.00 a square foot for the space. The broker, who was associated with a large, well-established firm, was so concerned about his credibility and reputation that he urgently tried to talk the tenant out of making such a ridiculous offer. In the end, the tenant secured the site at $2.07 per square foot. The negotiator offered other terms and incentives that the landlord found more meaningful than the actual rental rate. Had the negotiator heeded the broker's warning, he would have raised his initial offer to a more realistic $2.85, never knowing that $2.07 was the threshold.

Tough negotiating should not be confused with abusiveness. As representatives of a company, corporate negotiators are ambassadors. How they act partly determines the firm's public image. Aggressive negotiators who use bullying tactics or lies or are otherwise intimidating may make a few deals before their reputation precedes them. Then they will find that, because the real estate community is relatively small, transactions are becoming more difficult to put together. They may even find principals declining to meet with them and brokers unwilling to accept assignments.

Summing It Up

People function at differing levels of maturity. Stress, confrontation, or an otherwise threatening environment result in prompt regression to a basic, defensive, immature state of mind. The more relaxed and comfortable the negotiating environment, the better the communications between the parties. With improved communications, the parties will share needs, goals, and objectives. When people are relaxed, they are more inclined to view situations from alternative perspectives, which may allow for the creative solution of seemingly unsolvable problems.

In this posture it is easier to separate problems from conflicts and focus on alternative solutions. The primary task of all corporate negotiators is to understand the needs of the other party and to satisfy those needs without detriment to their own established company objectives, goals, or needs. True negotiators have a constructive attitude and work to build a strong, mutually supportive relationship that will result in a lasting agreement between the parties.

12
Office Leasing

Robert McLean, III
Senior Vice President, Cushman & Wakefield

Robert J. Sule
Vice President, Cushman & Wakefield

Step 1—Assign Full-Time Project Management

MR. SULE: When we embarked on our Phase 1 Corporate Housing Study in January of 1978, I decided, as the director of the real estate department at Dravo Corporation in Pittsburgh, that it would be important to involve various disciplines in the review process from the very outset. Since the implementation of any real estate strategy would have a profound impact on all of our people, it was essential to have the director of financial administration involved. To review the various financial implications of upgrading the space that we already occupied as compared with a new headquarters facility, we invited Chuck Strain, who had been with our finance department for a number of years. Our legal department was represented initially by our general counsel. As we got into prolonged lease negotiations, Jack Klee of that department became a key member of our four-member negotiating team.

Because our engineering task groups would occupy close to 70 percent of the space, we always involved a key member of that group in our monthly review meetings. And, finally, in order to assure good and regular communications with the corporate policy committee, the three top executives of Dravo attended all meetings and reported to the corporate policy committee as appropriate. This real estate committee, chaired by me, was to direct the life of our headquarters project over a five-year period.

MR. MCLEAN: We always advise our clients, whether involved in a major retrofit or a new facilities project, to form a building advisory committee or real estate committee similar to the one organized by Mr. Sule. The committee has two major responsibilities. The first is to review, approve, and monitor the schedule and the budget for the project. The second is to communicate effectively with, and to gain the support of, the entire company once the preferred alternative has been selected and is being implemented.

In order to accomplish this mission, the building advisory committee needs to be staffed by at least two full-time members. The first is the project manager, who has overall responsibility for all facets of the project, with particular emphasis on the delivery of all of the major base building systems. The second full-time staff member, who reports to the project manager, has primary responsibility for attending to the various user needs, including their present and future needs, the detailed layout of their space requirements, the stacking plan of corporate staff and other groups within the building envelope, the ordering of furniture systems, the move itself, and the postoccupancy interviews.

MR. SULE: When we realized in early 1978 that we should do some long-range planning and move to consolidate our fast-growing operations, which were at that time scattered at six locations, we knew that we would need outside consultant help. Apart from setting up our real estate committee, we wanted someone sitting next to us who had been involved in the planning and implementation of a number of headquarters facilities nationwide. We interviewed five firms and selected Cushman & Wakefield because they were becoming very active in Pittsburgh at that time and had worked with such companies as Bank of America, Sears, and ARCO in the planning and implementation of their high-rise office buildings. They were to assist us initially in the development of alternative real estate strategies, and once Dravo selected a new headquarters alternative, Cushman & Wakefield then assisted in the design and construction of the building itself and in the full lease and workletter negotiations.

MR. MCLEAN: Continuity is tremendously important to the successful planning and execution of a headquarters facility. Dravo was fortunate that its real estate committee for the most part consisted of the same people throughout the five-year period and, most importantly, its chairman remained the same over the entire life of the project. This continuity of leadership became even more important when the worldwide recession made it necessary for Dravo to effect a midcourse correction and swap their lease with the Mellon Bank. Working jointly and effectively with U.S. Steel, Dravo had created an institutional-quality building that was highly marketable to the Mellon Bank, whose growth was escalating as Dravo's was declining. Dravo's real estate management was able to effect a lease swap that was in the best interest of all parties.

Step 2—Audit Existing Facilities

MR. SULE: When Dravo began its preliminary feasibility studies in early 1978, the real estate committee was initially committed to making the "best case" for Dravo's consolidating in One Oliver Plaza and eventually growing into the building across the street, 300 6th Avenue. We instructed Cushman & Wakefield to make a thorough examination of all of the major systems in both buildings and to develop a preliminary budget of what it would cost to have the owner of those two buildings complete an upgrade to make the buildings state-of-the-art.

We also had our consultant team conduct interviews with 40 of our top corporate and operational managers to determine what Dravo's growth might be over a 20-year period and what would be the most efficient way of restacking our engineering task forces and the corporate support staff services so that we could conduct our business affairs in the most efficient and economic way within these two existing buildings. It was only after we felt comfortable that Dravo could renew its lease, undergo a retrofit, and grow into our existing space that we were prepared to enter the marketplace to see what competitive offers there might be from new building owners.

MR. MCLEAN: The development consultants of Cushman & Wakefield always advise our clients to conduct a thorough audit of their existing facilities and, for that matter, to see if a convincing case cannot be made for remaining and growing in its present quarters. It is only after a major space user has developed this database and this benchmark that management is really in a position to see how it compares with either building a new facility for their own account or looking for space in someone else's building. In the case of Dravo, this exercise turned out to be very beneficial, because as the Dravo real estate story unfolded, the firm finally decided to stay in a fully retrofitted One Oliver Plaza.

Step 3—View Alternatives in Terms of Expected Growth

MR. MCLEAN: Working with our own subsidiary, Building Programs International, and with any number of qualified space-planning firms, we have found that interviews with the top officers and divisional managers of a company develop essential information about their own views of how their present space helps or hinders the successful accomplishment of their business objectives, as well as what the anticipation of future personnel growth will be in terms of five-year plans and longer-range business objectives.

MR. SULE: In 1978, when the real estate committee reviewed low-, mid-, and high-range personnel projections, we were able to determine that the low projections could be accommodated in One Oliver Plaza and the building across the street, but the high projections would require space in a third building. At that particular time, we did not need or intend to sign a new lease, but we did feel it important to see what might be the best building profile if, in fact, the high projections turned out to be true as we moved toward our lease expiration in 1983.

Our consultants advised us that if we were to move into an ideal new building, the engineering task groups would be best accommodated on 40,000-square-foot floors and our corporate staff group on 20,000-square-foot floors. If the high projections turned out to be correct, we would need more than a million square feet over the next 20 years, of which 70,000 should be larger floors and 300,000 smaller floors. This, in fact, became a key ingredient when we subsequently developed a request for proposal and asked three competing developers to respond to these specific types of space requirements.

Step 4—Analyze Sites and Development Formats

MR. MCLEAN: During our work with several major office users in Pittsburgh, we had identified nine sites in the Golden Triangle and just across the rivers that had strong identity, the zoning capability, and the access and egress characteristics necessary for a major corporate headquarters building. In our initial interviews with the top officers and managers of these companies we reviewed the advantages and disadvantages of these nine sites with them and asked for their ranking of the sites in order of preference. As one might expect, there is always a very strong predilection to stay as close as possible to where you are. This was certainly the case with Dravo, whose top 40 executives almost unanimously selected the site right across the street from their present location at One Oliver Plaza and adjacent to Heinz Hall and Heinz Plaza.

MR. SULE: The problem that we had with the Heinz Hall site was that it did not provide the necessary floor plate of 40,000 square feet for our large engineering task groups. We had to move reluctantly from consideration of this location to two other sites on Grant Street, one a five-acre site owned by U.S. Steel and the other a two-acre site soon to be developed by the Oxford Development Company. At this preliminary stage, we felt that there would be a marvelous opportunity to influence both the design and construction of a headquarters building at either of these sites that could be custom-built to the Dravo requirement.

Working closely with our financial people, we had explored the various advantages and disadvantages of building for our own account, joint venturing, or being a tenant only. We concluded that if we could get a developer to custom-build a structure to our specific needs, we could report this as an operating lease, which would not have a significant impact on our balance sheet. This was the course we pursued.

MR. MCLEAN: There are a variety of financial options open to major users of office space. IBM, for example, has decided to joint venture office buildings in various cities where they occupy as much as half of the space. Some banks that we have worked with will take full responsibility for the design and construction of their headquarters facilities and then enter into a sale-lease-back of the property. The World Bank in Washington, which occupies over 3 million square feet of space and is a tax-exempt organization, has decided to maintain the ownership of most of its office space because of the tax implications. Each institution has to weigh the various tax, balance-sheet, and risk issues involved in ownership, joint-venture, and tenant-only formats and arrive at a decision that meets their specific objectives.

Step 5—Prepare Building Package

MR. SULE: Early in 1978, the Pittsburgh real estate market was in a formative and competitive period. Several developers who had recently gained control of very attractive sites were searching for anchor tenants that would enable their projects to move forward. In light of these circumstances, our real estate committee instructed the consultant team to put together a detailed request for proposals. This building package described the type of architectural statement Dravo wanted to make with its headquarters building, the sizes and amounts of space that Dravo would need over a 25-year lease term, detailed specifications of the quality level of all of the major building systems, and special requirements such as a mail conveyor system, a heliport, an auditorium, and a cafeteria. Each developer was invited to render a schematic of a Dravo headquarters building at their site and to detail all the particulars of a long-term lease for Dravo as a tenant.

MR. MCLEAN: The major point developed in my recent book, *Countdown to Renaissance II, The New Way Corporate America Builds,* is the entirely different manner in which corporations plan their headquarters facilities today as compared to years gone by. For example, after the Second World War and even up until recent times, many developers would select favorable sites, construct high-rise buildings, and, while in the process of construction, look for tenants. Today, making use of the strategic planning process, corporations are much more prone to develop a building package such as Dravo did and then go to the marketplace to have developers respond specifically to that building package. The results are buildings that not only respond specifically to user need but also fit into and enrich the urban landscape. Pittsburgh's new Renaissance II skyline is a marvelous example of this approach.

Step 6—Establish Schedule, Budget, and Teams

MR. MCLEAN: Once a site has been selected and a schematic for the project endorsed, it is essential for the team, the owner's representative, and the development consultant to adopt a preliminary budget and schedule for the project, both the base building construction and the interior fit-out. It is then important for the team to review and fine-tune that budget and schedule monthly and to make necessary revisions and updates as required.

MR. SULE: In establishing my project organization for the Dravo Tower, I assigned a full-time person to be the project manager with primary responsibilities for the monitoring of the base building construction. Reporting directly to him was another person who had primary responsibilities for the Dravo interior fit-out of 612,000 square feet. I then looked to our consulting team, Cushman & Wakefield and Gibbs and Hill, to provide day-to-day support in keeping the project on budget and on schedule. The real estate committee, which I chaired, would meet monthly to receive a status report and to resolve problems. As required, we would go to the corporate policy committee and board for major budget approvals.

Step 7—Negotiate Master Lease

MR. SULE: When the decision was made in February 1980 to go to the U.S. Steel site, a memorandum of understanding was signed by the principals, which approved construction costs for rental purposes but left open permanent financing costs until they were secured. The memorandum also addressed the amounts of space and the quality of construction, but as might be expected, a number of details, such as options to expand, sublet provisions, and cleaning specifications, were left on the table to be negotiated.

I decided that we should set up a small negotiating team made up of myself, a real estate associate from Dravo, someone from our legal department, and Bob McLean from Cushman & Wakefield. We were given full authority by the executive office to move these negotiations forward within clearly established guidelines. U.S. Steel set up a similar team headed by the newly appointed president of the U.S. Steel Realty Group. Some two years later, when the building was virtually complete, the 250-page lease document was finally ready for signature by both parties. It was executed in July 1982.

MR. MCLEAN: Four issues were particularly noteworthy in the Dravo/U.S. Steel lease negotiations.

The first was Dravo's ability to grow at a rather rapid rate into the balance of the building. The initial occupancy would be approximately 600,000 square feet, but we saw the need over the next 20 years for Dravo's occupying another 600,000 square feet, leaving a balance of only 200,000 square feet in the remainder of the building. In the beginning of our lease negotiations, Dravo was on a tremendous growth path, and we saw the need for at least 120,000 feet of additional space five years after move-in. This obviously presented problems to U.S. Steel, which saw the difficulty of leasing 120,000 feet for a five-year term.

The second issue related to Dravo's ability to sublet space, particularly space in the base of the building, where their engineering task groups would be located on 40,000-foot floors. The ebb and tide of Dravo's engineering business indicated that there might be times when one, two, or three of these floors might be available for sublet over a short period of time. Dravo felt that any profits that might accrue from this sublet should be for their own account. U.S. Steel saw this possible sublet activity as being competitive with other space that might be available in that building, and they felt that any profits should accrue to them.

The third issue related to the quality of cleaning in the building. Dravo would not be managing the building but would be occupying initially half the space and eventually most of the space. They felt it appropriate that they have some control over the day-to-day cleaning of their quarters.

The fourth issue related to overtime charges for air-conditioning. In many of Dravo's engineering assignments they were on a fast-track schedule, and major task force groups of 400 or 500 people would often have to work overtime in order to meet various project schedules. During the spring, summer, and fall months, this would often involve calling for back-up air-conditioning after normal business hours. The Dravo negotiating team felt that it would be appropriate to pay for this after-hours air-conditioning at cost. U.S. Steel maintained that there were standard hourly charges for after-hours air-conditioning and that those standard charges would be appropriate for Dravo as well as other tenants.

It was only after major concessions were granted in these four areas that the Dravo negotiating team recommended that the lease document be signed.

Step 8—Monitor Building Construction

MR. MCLEAN: One of the major responsibilities of our development consultants group is to monitor base building construction daily to make sure that specifications are met and the schedule is maintained. This pertains not only to base building construction but also to tenant work to assure that floors are turned over to the tenant as scheduled and that move-in can take place in an orderly and successful manner.

MR. SULE: During the course of construction of the Dravo Tower over a 30-month period, we looked to Cushman & Wakefield to formally report to us on a monthly basis on the status of the buy-outs of the major building systems and for confirmation that the quality standards established in our initial request for proposal were being fully met. Indeed, Cushman & Wakefield really became an extension of my staff and worked alongside my project manager, reporting to him on a daily basis.

We had assembled our own team of Swanke, Hayden and Connell and our own subsidiary, Gibbs and Hill, to develop the full architectural plans for our tenant fit-out work. Because we were moving from primarily closed offices to an open plan, we felt it most important to develop a mock-up of how our space would look after we actually moved into the Dravo Tower, so that all of our employees could see firsthand the various furniture systems that we would be utilizing and become accustomed to, and comfortable with, the new work stations in our headquarters facility. This mock-up of 12,000 square feet of actual conditions in the new building became an extremely important educational and promotional tool to prepare our people for the new work environment.

Step 9—Effect Midcourse Corrections

MR. MCLEAN: We have always advised our clients to develop the best case for remaining and expanding in their present quarters as compared with the best case for moving to a new facility designed and constructed around their specific needs. In our work with PPG and Dravo in Pittsburgh, we developed a viable case for both firms to remain in retrofitted facilities, where they had lived happily for many years. As they both compared this alternative with the possibility of moving to a new headquarters facility at several available sites in the downtown area, they always knew that they could return to the safe harbor of where they were. In the case of Dravo, unpredictable business conditions and a worldwide recession led the firm to swap its lease with the Mellon Bank, which was growing fast, and to remain in a fully retrofitted One Oliver Plaza, which our early studies had shown would be a viable alternative.

MR. SULE: In 1978, when all of us at Dravo were in a very robust mood about the future and we saw an opportunity to take advantage of a very competitive marketplace, it seemed foolish to some of us to spend so much time looking at the alternative of remaining where we were. I often asked myself why we were taking the time and spending the money to have these Cushman & Wakefield people look at the skin of the building to see where the leaks were, standing on top of elevator cabs to see the quality of the core cinder block construction, and checking the various life safety systems. As far as I was concerned, we should have been concentrating on a new building solution. In retrospect, I realize how important all that early work was to establish both the cost and the program to upgrade the building we were in.

MR. MCLEAN: Incidentally, the same kind of strategic planning was also very helpful to the Mellon Bank. We conducted interviews with their top 60 officers in mid-1979 as well as an audit of the long-term adequacy of their existing space. These studies determined that their growth might well involve doubling their space requirements over the next 10 years. This information was reviewed and endorsed by their corporate office, first in 1980 and again in 1981. Having carefully reviewed and affirmed this kind of growth, Mellon was positioned well to move aggressively when the Dravo Tower became available in the latter part of 1982.

There is no question that the use of strategic planning and the establishment of a detailed database enable corporations such as Dravo and the Mellon Bank to effect appropriate midcourse corrections as changes occur in their business operations and in the marketplace.

Step 10—Conduct
Postoccupancy Interviews

MR. MCLEAN: Long after the architect has won a design award for the building, the general contractor has gone over his last punch list, and the developer is receiving his monthly rental payments, the occupants of the office space are either working productively or not so efficiently in the workstations and environments that have been designed and constructed for them. That is why we have always recommended to our clients that within a year of occupancy they take the time to interview their employees to see if the original objectives established for the new building have been met. These postoccupancy interviews relate to such matters as lighting and glare, acoustics, circulation, workflow, conferencing, telecommunications, colors, warmth, and informal networking. The interviews provide important feedback to management about how the space is perceived by the employees, demonstrate that management has in mind both the comfort and productivity of its people, and enable management to change such things as circulation and lighting, if changes are in fact required.

MR. SULE: I think the greatest lesson that our real estate committee learned, apart from being flexible and effecting midcourse corrections, was the importance of involving our employees in the planning process. It is more of an art form than a science. On the one hand, management needs to establish guidelines and workstation standards that provide necessary order and discipline to the corporation. On the other hand, to develop high morale, participation, and support, it is necessary for management both to involve and to inform all its employees in a positive manner in the planning and execution of either new or retrofitted quarters.

We found the mock-up of our new workstation standards to be a marvelous middle ground, where both the objectives of management and the participation of employees could meet and be accommodated. It also became the proving ground where the real estate committee could examine firsthand the furniture systems of various suppliers and narrow the options. It was both a good selection tool for our real estate committee and an educational vehicle for all of our employees.

MR. MCLEAN: Dravo followed the 10-point development process that corporations, using the strategic planning process, and the development community, responding to dramatic changes in building and office technology, have jointly perfected in recent years. The 10 steps described here provide a road map that creates not only custom-made facilities delivered on time and on budget but also facilities that nourish and enliven the urban marketplace.

13
Retail Site Selection

David P. Segal

Vice President, Corporate Real Estate, Dunkin' Donuts

Finding locations for McDonald's is the most creatively fulfilling thing I can imagine. I go out and check out a piece of property. It's nothing but bare ground, not producing a damned thing for anybody. I put a building on it, and the operator gets into business there employing fifty or a hundred people, and there is new business for the garbage man, the landscape man, and the people who sell the meat and buns and potatoes and other things. So out of that bare piece of ground comes a store that does, say, a million dollars a year in business. Let me tell you, it's a great satisfaction to see that happen.[1]

Successful companies use different concepts and guidelines to select locations for their businesses. Before describing specific guidelines for selecting good locations, we must first consider the latest scientific methods of analyzing and forecasting sales, the indispensable role of good judgment and experience, and the many myths and pitfalls of location selection.

Is Site Selection an Art or a Science?

In the 1960s and 1970s, experienced and successful site selectors typically were not scientific in their approach. They would identify a promising loca-

---

[1] From Ray Kroc and Robert Anderson, *Grinding It Out: The Making of McDonald's,* Berkley Publishing, New York, 1982.

tion, explore the area with only street maps to guide them, and visit places people go—the local supermarkets, restaurants, and bars. They would talk with office workers, shippers in the nearest industrial area, and even the police or firemen. In short, site selectors evaluated potential locations primarily by mingling with people, listening to them talk about the community, and observing where they came from and where they went.

Numerous attempts were made to understand scientifically more about potential customers. However, readily available demographic data often failed to reveal the reasons for location success or failure. By 1980, a number of companies were using computers to generate market surveys. These modern systems, however, were costly and caused many companies to become overly dependent on the consultants who sold computer services. In many cases computer use did not improve the predictability of sales. Indeed, in some companies where computers were imposed on seasoned site selectors, without properly involving them in the planning and use of the new systems, highly skilled executives lost motivation and not infrequently resigned. Whatever was gained by scientific analysis was offset by a decline in overall field organization productivity. In a 1979 TV interview, Ray Kroc suggested how to solve this problem. He acknowledged that we need computers but cautioned that they will never replace "gut feel."

What do we mean by "gut feel"? One definition is that it is simply when you begin to feel what's right. For some businesses, on the other hand, scientific methods, computers, regression analysis, and modeling can narrow the risk of site selection. This is particularly the case when businesses such as supermarkets, convenience food stores, banks, shoe stores, bakeries, and other retailers generate sales from customers whose buying trips are planned.

In 1984, Tom Gay, executive vice president of Marketing Information Systems (MIS), of Encinitas, California, which sells a computerized site-selection and sales-forecasting service, said, "Overall we agree for the most part with the need for a site selection specialist to have experience and use judgment in the process of evaluating a location. Sales forecasts for practically every site need an adjustment factor. Based on experience, the final computerized sales forecast needs a gut-feel adjustment to reflect special circumstances that are beyond the computer's capacity."

Examples abound of the interrelationship of scientific analysis and good judgment:

Population and Demography

Successful application of the scientific site-selection process is illustrated by John Thompson, of Thompson Associates Marketing Research, Los Altos, California. One of Thompson's clients, a home improvement chain, located stores in markets with a large number of senior citizens. The disappointing sales experience of these stores was attributed to the predominance of senior citizens in these markets. At first blush this was a plausible theory because per capita expenditures for home improvement items were lower for seniors than for younger consumers. Thompson, however, found another answer. He prepared a sales-forecasting model using a database of stores in trade areas, including both a high and a low percentage of seniors. From this model he concluded that age did not explain differences in sales volume. Instead, housing types—the proportion of single-family, multifamily-rental, condominium, and mobile homes—determined sales.

He then demonstrated that not only did single-family residents spend about five times more than multifamily dwellers at home improvement centers but sales decreased as store distances increased.

Thompson probed deeper by working closely with experienced executives in the chain's real estate department. They concluded that for contractors the location of job sites determined levels of spending at home improvement centers. Thompson and his clients came to understand that where people were going could be even more important than where they lived.

Another example of the relative importance of demography and destination was described by the senior vice president of a major drug and cosmetic chain in New England. He pointed out that cosmetic sales vary with ethnic groups (e.g., Jewish and Italian populations are relatively greater consumers of cosmetics). However, regardless of demography, it is better to place drugstores near hospitals, medical offices, and health clubs. Some drugstore chains choose locations in malls, depending on the nature and size of the key traffic generators in the mall. Here again, destination is often more important than where customers live.

Traffic and Road Configuration

Both the computer and the flesh-and-blood site analyst must contend with the misleading nature of traffic counts. If vehicles travel on a road for relatively long distances—usually over three miles—there is a greater portion of transient traffic on that road. Generally, the longer the road, the more transient the traffic. Conversely, the shorter the road, the more local the traffic. People traveling locally tend to drive both ways on the same road and sometimes pass by the same location several times in one day. Thus local traffic, which tends to exaggerate the number of potential customers passing a location, can cause an error by either the individual site selector or the computer.

In almost all cases, roads with state or interstate route numbers are transient roads. Roads with county route numbers, roads with no route numbers, roads that are relatively narrow, or roads that have been bypassed by highways are usually local, except at those points where there are important traffic generators and dense populations. The possible exceptions are "Broadways" and "Main Streets," which are relatively long and wide. The distribution of transient and local traffic is best determined by studying maps and noting the strategic reach of key roads. It is also possible to assess the transient or local nature of a road by following groups of cars and observing how far they go before turning off. The computer cannot do this.

To measure the importance of the total traffic count, therefore, it is essential to know the nature of the traffic (local or transient), the characteristics of the business, and the degree to which its customers plan their purchases or simply buy on impulse. Generally, more impulse business will come from transient roads, more planned purchases from local roads. Because most roads carry some transient and some local traffic, experience and judgment are vitally important in the evaluation of any site.

Possible road changes must also be considered. If a road is bypassed, for example, then it will lose much of its transient traffic. On the other hand, where major traffic generators develop later, the bypass may actually cause transient traffic to increase by making it easy for transient traffic to reach the traffic generators.

Trade Areas

In order to measure site potential, or how many shops should be located in a market, especially if a business requires a significant number of impulse customers, it is necessary to measure the potential of traffic generators. A coffee shop's business, for example, will vary, depending on the nearest department store and other retailers. Where they are located in relation to interstate highways and population concentrations and the extent to which those department stores and other retailers advertise regionally are also factors. Any study of site potential, therefore, must also address these factors.

Parking

The sales impact of parking spaces is complicated and usually is evaluated best by individuals who have observed a large variety of parking conditions. Street parking and encroachment by others, for example, must be understood. Customer access from nearby parking lots may be a factor. It is also necessary to judge the extent to which parking convenience is important to customers, especially for those businesses where the typical sale is small. Because of these complications, and the fact that certain high-volume shops may have small parking lots while low-volume shops may have large parking lots, modeling often falsely indicates that parking does not have an impact on sales. However, common sense suggests that it must be taken seriously.

Competition (Numbers, Quality, and Location)

Direct and indirect competition almost always appear as components in a sales-forecasting formula. Because competitors have varying degrees of strength, however, they should be classified to determine actual impact. If one competitor averages $1.3 million per location and another $1 million, the first may be in class A and the latter in class B, with a further variable added for relative location in the market. Indirect competition—similar but not identical operations—must also be considered.

Competition comes in different forms. Two freestanding drugstores in a local community, for example, are in direct competition with each other. Supermarkets, however, which carry many of the drugstore products, are indirect competitors. Although these competitors can be identified objectively, their impact will depend on certain variables, the significance of which will be apparent only to one who has had experience evaluating them.

If most customers stop at a location on impulse, then the direct or indirect competitor with the best location has an advantage. If purchases are planned, advertising and market strength provide an advantage. Sometimes, however, location and competition do not decide success or failure. Dave Ferron, former vice president of Consumer Value Stores, tells the story of a town in which several drugstores in "fairly good" locations were doing poorly while one independent druggist in a poor location did well. The reason was that the independent had a close relationship with the union members of the largest employer in town and had arranged for prescription payments by the union directly to that druggist. Contacts and creative marketing can sometimes overcome location disadvantages. The computer cannot deal with these kinds of unique circumstances.

Central Business District

The site selector must determine the nature of the central business district. For example, there are differences between a rural county seat and a satellite town. The county seat usually draws from a large area, which often encompasses a number of towns. The county seat would, therefore, have a larger portion of transient traffic than a satellite town.

Activity Quality and Compatibility

Within each category of traffic generators there are different degrees of drawing power. Certain supermarket chains, for example, usually draw better than others. Local promotions and prices, advertising strength, trademark value, the number of strategic locations, and operational quality are responsible for this. A good site analyst can weight these nonquantifiable factors, a regression model cannot.

Depending on their characteristics, traffic generators and competitors have different effects on a business. A mall, for example, may be a large traffic generator. It may have an adverse impact on a nearby restaurant or retailer, however, if similar operations are in the mall. On the other hand, shopping centers, hospitals, banks, offices, and theaters reinforce each other and support a large variety of nearby small and medium-size businesses. Retailers selling natural foods and health products do better near health clubs, not near ice cream or pizza shops. Paint stores do well on roads heavily traveled by men or near home improvement centers. Banks like to establish themselves in growth markets, because the decision to open a bank account is usually a long-term one. People are reluctant to change banks once the relationship is established. Ice cream, bakery, and candy shops, however, may not be compatible near each other, especially in smaller markets.

Other Strategic Factors

Also important in determining store placement is the marketing strategy, which includes advertising, local market strength, and the number of sites needed to fully penetrate a market. The computer cannot model these circumstances by itself. Human judgment is needed to put these factors in perspective.

In general, many site selection judgments require a combination of experience and common sense, which cannot be measured accurately by a computer. The proper use of computers can often help evaluate a market and a location, but only a flesh-and-blood site selector can arrive at a decision. Computers are no magical panacea. You, the site selector, must come up with the answer. The decision is yours—a judgment call. Site selection is still an art, an art assisted by technology.

The Myths of Site Selection

As with any art form, there are a great many myths associated with site selection which can negatively affect your judgment. Avoid these common fallacies:

Proximity of Locations Diminishes Sales

How close should shops be placed to each other? Many circumstances determine the proximity of shops. In the Dunkin' Donuts chain, for example, relatively high average sales have resulted from concentrated shop placement. In the Manchester, New Hampshire, Standard Metropolitan Statistical Area (SMSA) in 1984 there were nine shops covering a total of 173,630 people, or 19,290 per shop. In Providence, Rhode Island, there were 36 shops per 919,220 people, or 25,530 people per shop. In some cases, shops were placed less than a mile apart. In Hartford, Connecticut, there are two outlets within 300 feet of each other. One obtains substantial support from the Hartford Civic Center, nearby offices, and retail shops, the other from the activity generated by adjoining shops and offices. In the Pennsylvania Railroad Station in New York City there are four outlets within 200 feet, covering different pedestrian traffic flows. On the other hand, Dunkin' Donuts executives would acknowledge that in a small town or in a suburban area there may be considerably more people per shop because of the limited number of traffic generators and because of the nature of the traffic flows.

Thus retail shops and restaurants, which are very dependent on impulse business, rely on other traffic generators. In order to determine how close together to place units in the market, it is necessary to understand the trade area of the traffic generators.

To repeat, a survey is needed to identify not only where customers live or are coming from but, more importantly, where they are going. A survey often reveals that many customers of a chain of shops in a given area actually live closer to other units of the same chain. Franchise owners or managers often complain that a proposed new store would be too close to their location because the people who live near the proposed unit are already their customers. Their argument, however, is often unfounded because the pattern of impulse shopping may depend on where people are going rather than where they live. If the existing shop is nearest the traffic generator, then another unit located where the people live would not take away the impulse buyer, whose primary objective is the generator.

On the other hand, the placement of new shops in relation to existing units may affect the existing customer who plans purchases beforehand. Assuming equal operational standards and prices, customers will go directly to the nearest location to make their purchases. In this case, the location itself is the traffic generator, and its customers will go to the outlet that is easiest to reach. It is important to note, however, that because of trademark dynamics and more advertising generated by greater density of shops in the marketplace, the competition of multiple locations is usually offset by the increased awareness of the chain that results from greater exposure of the name and business concept in the market. The Dunkin' Donuts experience in Manchester, Providence, and other markets illustrates this concept well.

Impulse and Planned Purchase Customers Involve Equal Predictability

From a market research perspective, it is not difficult to measure the potential business that could come from customers who plan their purchases in advance, especially the purchase of staple items. The supermarket and convenience-food researchers, for example, have a good track record in measuring this kind of potential. Their task is relatively simple because they sell necessities, the constant consumption of which is known statistically. Relevant population and demographic data are also readily available. This purchasing predictability explains why there are relatively few failures in these businesses.

The problem of dealing with impulse and planned purchase customers is complicated when a business appeals to both types. A coffee shop, for example, is substantially impulse-oriented, especially during the morning and late evening hours. However, if the coffee shop adds a bakery, it will also depend on planned purchases. In this case, much of the morning business will depend on where people are going, which is more difficult to evaluate; the afternoon and evening business will depend mostly on where people live, which is less difficult to evaluate.

The Larger the Population and the Traffic Volume, the Better

A larger population and traffic volume does little good if the road is diverted and it bypasses your location. It is better to be located between where customers live and downtown, other traffic generators, or access-ways to major roads. It is unprofitable to have an impulse-dependent business, such as a convenience restaurant, on the edge of town beyond traffic generators or strategic points.

The impact of traffic volume depends upon such factors as typical speed, access, road configuration (e.g., width, dividers, traffic controls), and traffic mix (i.e., local versus transient, trucks versus cars). Also important is the visual character of the area—clutter, signage, and obstructions.

You Get What You Pay For in Choosing Locations

Each location is unique. Sometimes a location is expensive because the owner is a tough negotiator or because of improper appraisal or because it is more suitable to a higher use, for example, a large office building. A company may also choose to overpay, if necessary, because the property is needed to satisfy corporate objectives.

The Far Corner Is Best

This is only true if that corner is at an intersection where it is most visible and accessible. The near corner may be just as good, or even better, depending upon the importance of the cross street at that intersection.

It Is Wise to "Icebox" (Land Bank) Locations

In the 1950s and 1960s, many oil companies did this to procure service station locations and found either that they were paying tomorrow's prices today or that the area did not develop as anticipated.

Competition Is Bad

Some concepts do better near competitors, especially those businesses where consumers usually shop to compare values (e.g., automobile dealers, furniture, and clothing). Although restaurants usually compete for a limited number of customers, there are exceptions. Certain hamburger chains, for example, will occasionally take a location near a high-volume competitor with limited parking. Food courts in large shopping malls may also attract more combined customers than the individual competitor restaurants could draw on their own.

Traffic Counts in Cities throughout the United States Are Generally of Similar Value if the Traffic Counts Are Similar

Cities in the South or West were often better planned from a traffic standpoint than those in the Northeast. These better-planned cities generally were designed with a road grid to avoid congestion and to allow better movement of traffic. These patterns are good for destination businesses such as tablecloth restaurants and major retailers. However, the consequence of these grid patterns is to minimize the availability of key strategic locations with a good transient mix, which is essential for many retail and restaurant operations dependent on impulse buying.

Good Signs and Bold Colors Are Enough

It is the total image of the site, not good signs or bold colors, that is important. Lack of visibility, poor access, fast traffic, poorly maintained property, or an unattractive setting can overwhelm even the best signage.

Landscaping Is Low Priority

In the early 1960s, McDonald's determined that not only were the yellow arches and the garish red-and-white buildings causing them to lose locations in zoning and permit processes but those designs were actually not appealing to most customers. Management changed to natural woods and dark brick and, most important, accented well-planned landscaping. The McDonald's image was thus changed from a drive-in to a family-style restaurant and, largely because of this new image, expansion accelerated.

Pitfalls

In addition to avoiding overreliance on computer models and ignoring the mythology described above, the good site selector must watch out for certain pitfalls.

The Numbers Game

Companies need quality, not just quantity, of locations. The importance of finding *successful* locations is too often underemphasized by top management. A sense of timing is critical when developing new sites. Each market can absorb additional units at a different rate, depending on regional economic conditions, local market strength, competition, proximity, saturation, availability of good sites, and the ability of operations personnel to manage or supervise new units. Excessive pressure to multiply locations forces the field organization to compromise on site selection and negotiations. People selecting locations need time to develop alternatives and a reliable supply of prospective locations.

Dependence on Traffic Generators

It is a mistake to rely on just a few traffic generators. Situations change. A military base may relocate or reduce operations; an employment center may close. Roads lose traffic when bypassed by an interstate highway. It is also a mistake to rely on anticipated changes. A shopping center that is "coming soon," for example, may never open or, if it does, may not provide the anticipated draw.

Following the Leaders

Everyone's concept is different. It is usually good to be where others are busy, but watch out for subtle differences and the possibility that even the most successful companies sometimes make mistakes.

Taking Honesty for Granted

Knowledgeable management can detect activity that is unethical or even illegal among their field representatives. A great deal of money is involved in putting together real estate deals. People in the field are usually working with brokers, developers, and landowners without close supervision, and there are frequent opportunities for corruption.

An experienced manager will notice the telltale signs of corruption: low productivity, expensive deals, close relationships between a field representative and relatively few brokers, a pattern of acquisitions involving simultaneous closings, and title reports showing recent changes of ownership.

Ignoring the Complexities of the Market Plan

There is a tendency to rely too heavily on published statistical data and not enough on the unique characteristics of the local market or actual sales experience in different markets. Nevertheless, in new markets the first step in preparing for expansion is to obtain information and statistics from available market reports or from consultants. These data can help rank each market in terms of consumption, competition, media, and cost of doing business.

The market plan must also coordinate corporate functions—marketing and operations—with analysis by the real estate field organization. Operations executives, for example, will best understand the relative profitability of local markets. They can estimate what positive or negative effects would result from the addition of new units. Marketing executives can determine the affordability and impact of advertising for new shops. The construction department can project building costs and schedules. Site selectors must evaluate this information carefully and then determine where they can secure good locations, given the limitations imposed by operating, marketing, and construction considerations.

The Larger Perspective

The relative importance of the concepts dealt with in this chapter will, of course, vary by industry and by company. Each site selector must understand the exceptions that are encountered in the field and how they affect the particular assignment at hand. Although no two firms have identical objectives and circumstances, the following general principles will nearly always apply:

- Listen to the consumers. Identify who they are, where they live, and where they go.

- Research the markets. Seek out the best opportunity areas by combining sound real estate judgment with sophisticated decision-making tools that are designed to reduce the risks inherent in market expansion.

- Study the company's strengths and weaknesses and those of direct and indirect competitors.

- Use computer technology, sometimes with the help of consultants, to analyze geographic and demographic statistics. But do not underestimate the experience of executives who must apply the information and the company's resources on a practical basis.

- If you have a model and a sales-forecasting mechanism, make sure their limits are understood by all users.

- Keep good records and continuously make improvements by critiquing successes as well as failures.

- Attract into the real estate department honest and dedicated people with talent and an entrepreneurial spirit.

- Work with a sense of urgency to excel. This is measured in terms of sales of new units and shop profits plus individual and overall organization productivity.

- Put the organization and a team effort before personal interests.

- Never be content.

- Negotiate carefully. Line up alternative locations to strengthen bargaining positions. Prepare well. Have patience and sensitivity.

- Never forget the principles laid down by the founders of the company, but be prepared for change. Regardless of your company's product, service, or sphere of operations, these principles will serve you and your company well.

14

Asset Disposition

Bernard P. Giroux

Vice President, Marketing, Marathon U.S. Realties, Inc.

The Disposition Process

Disposing of Real Estate

The disposition or redeployment of real estate assets has been an important corporate topic for at least the last 10 years, as senior managers have come to understand the revenue that can be generated from surplus or underutilized property. It is a complicated subject. No two disposition situations are identical. There are, however, certain guidelines that apply to most dispositions, which are discussed in this essay.

Sources of Assets for Disposition

The major reason for disposing of assets is discontinued operations. Corporations discontinue operations for several reasons. The first is market withdrawal. A good example of market withdrawal was the cessation of operations by much of the textile industry in New England after World War II. Textile operators moved their plants to southern states, creating enormous inventories of vacant multistory manufacturing and warehouse space throughout New England. Because most of this production space was leased, it left owners with special-purpose buildings and no market for them. A second relocation wave has hit the textile industry with the availability of inexpensive labor in the Pacific Rim nations. Textiles have moved offshore, once again leaving behind assets for disposition due to discontinued operations.

Market withdrawals are also visible in the retail sector. The Great Atlantic & Pacific Tea Company and other national supermarket chains retrenched heavily in the early 1970s. Marketing areas shrunk by divisions and there was wholesale closure of facilities throughout the United States. Similarly, the oil companies eliminated many uneconomical service stations in the 1970s.

Another reason for disposition occurs when operations are consolidated. Surplus facilities are created, for example, when the government closes installations in order to consolidate or eliminate redundant or unnecessary functions. Corporations encounter similar disposition circumstances when scattered facilities are consolidated into fewer modern and efficient locations. Financial organizations may move "back-room" operations from high-cost, central-city locations to lower-cost locations outside of a central business district. A retail facility may be located in an obsolete building, prompting the development of a new facility in a more desirable location. This same scenario may be repeated for any organization, large or small.

Liquidations are the most compelling reason for dispositions. The ability to generate profits or maximize returns from real estate being liquidated is usually lost to the seller, but the skillful sale or lease of real estate assets can significantly improve the liquidation value of the company, in some instances giving rise to new enterprise.

Asset disposition requires management, whether the asset manager is disposing of a single facility or an entire real estate portfolio. Every opportunity to generate profitable dispositions should be exploited. Dispositions are not yard sales.

Survey of Assets

In order to properly manage the disposition of corporate facilities, an up-to-date survey of the assets is needed. The condition of each facility should be precisely understood. Leased property should be described and a copy of all leases with current amendments or ancillary documents should be available. A department store lease, for example, should have the reciprocal operating agreement attached. Retail facilities with percentage rent clauses should have the records of percentage rent payments.

The real estate disposition manager should personally inspect each facility. This provides the basis for a detailed physical description, an estimate of deferred maintenance, an evaluation of functional or physical obsolescence and economic obsolescence, and a rating of the location. Disposition cannot be managed from an armchair.

The corporate real estate manager should be principally responsible for asset disposition. This should not be left to brokers or other consultants, although their assistance may be valuable. This is integral to the asset management role. With proper knowledge of the inventory to be disposed of, a good knowledge of the real estate business, and the ability to visualize multiple uses for property, the real estate manager can orchestrate the disposition of assets profitably.

Marketing Assets for Disposition

The disposition of assets requires a plan that has a clearly defined purpose and objective. It should be results-oriented and should attempt to maximize whatever benefits are available to the corporation.

Realities of the Marketplace

General economic and market conditions will have an effect on disposition of corporate real estate. The type of facility which is being disposed of is also a factor. The age, location, condition, and size of a facility will dictate the results of the disposition. A major U.S. retail company, for example, owned a 50-year-old multistory distribution and retail complex in a large midwestern city. The location was valuable in every respect, with interstate access, a 30-acre-plus site, and a surrounding middle-income population of sufficient density to warrant large-scale retail development. The corporation thought that the location had a value slightly in excess of $20 million. However, the market-driven course of action was to demolish the facility, add to the land area by further assemblage, and develop a much larger shopping center on the site. The costs of performing this type of complex development work were little understood in the company. A developer would need five to eight years to complete the assemblage, demolition, reconstruction, and occupancy of a new facility. This meant that the developer would be willing to pay no more than $16 million for this location.

In another example, a consultant advised a national supermarket chain to dispose of its discontinued stores wholesale, without evaluating the real estate potential of each site. More than 4000 locations had been disposed of before management finally realized that it was giving away substantial subleasing profits. Its retail space had an average term of 10 years remaining on leases, with three or more five-year options on each lease at similar base rents. Gross rents averaged $2.25 per square foot in markets where similar space leased for $2.75 to $4.75 net. With its remaining 2000 locations the corporation began to make significant subleasing profits. The market, in short, may dictate less than corporate assumptions, as in the first example, or it may dictate more, as in the second example.

Under different circumstances, the real estate manager may create value using existing assets. A company in New York City enlarged a retail facility on Broadway on the Upper West Side. It expanded the building footprint from about 1300 square feet to 24,000 square feet. The corporate real estate manager, however, realized that the single-story retail facility was an underutilization of the land. A sale-leaseback was created with one of New York's foremost apartment developers. The site was sold for $175 per square foot—five times the book value. In return, the corporation received a lease for a new, slightly smaller retail facility at below-market rates for 40 years, which was built into the high-rise condominium developed on the site. Additionally, the retail firm obtained a 25 percent limited partnership interest in the $75 million high-rise project.

The implementation of a disposition plan requires the corporate manager to be involved completely in the marketing of the property. Corporate management must give the real estate manager the flexibility needed to maximize disposition alternatives. A disposition plan must provide for unexpected contingencies. It must be broad enough to accommodate changing market realities.

Plan Implementation

There are several elements required in carrying out a disposition plan. The degree to which they are used will vary depending on the type of facility and its location, age, and value.

Valuation

Each property to be disposed of should be appraised. The appraiser should discuss the following subjects thoroughly:

1. *Location and analysis.* A comprehensive analysis of location and competing sites is necessary to evaluate the probable success of the disposition. The market elements will give an idea of the timetable.

2. *Zoning.* After a complete synopsis of the property's zoning, alternatives to the existing use should be analyzed, if appropriate.

3. *Physical description.* The appraiser should present an objective, detailed description of the property for the benefit of management and

include all visible elements of deferred maintenance or forms of obsolescence.

4. *Alternative uses.*   If applicable, the appraiser should condition the evaluation, depending upon alternative uses that may be available for the property. This will affect the final value conclusions. The appraisal should be used as a tool in the disposition process. It presents the real estate manager with a single, comprehensive document listing the important variables of the property that assist in its marketing.

Engineering Reports

In the sale of major facilities, engineering studies are often required. These reports should be performed by qualified outside engineering firms to give the corporate manager and potential buyers a clear picture of the physical status of the facility. Engineering reports are detailed; they are often technical and require interpretation. At times they can have a negative effect on the disposition plan, but they are needed and should cover these issues:

1. *Roofs.*   Roofs are a primary source of difficulty in all major structures. They require considerable capital for repair or replacement.

2. *Heating, ventilation, and air-conditioning.*   All elements of an HVAC system are important for maintaining an adequate working environment in any facility. Specific review and recommendations of all these systems should be made in an engineering report. The report should stress age, condition, repairs, and replacement of equipment that may be required.

3. *Utilities.*   Domestic, commercial, and industrial services should be examined. Building equipment design and capacities are important elements of any analysis. Sprinkler systems should be part of this analysis, too. Are utilities over or under capacity for certain uses?

4. *Structure.*   Detailed structural analyses will reveal important features of a building. Some structural problems are not readily apparent. On the West Coast, older structures need to be examined for earthquake code compliance. In Portland, Oregon, a 50-year-old multistory industrial structure was examined for earthquake resistance. The structure had only minor noncompliance items because the method of construction at the time tied the walls and floors to the columns. This was a poured-in-place reinforced-concrete structure. It was a massive building that had been through many earthquakes with no apparent damage or flaws. This is an extreme example, but depending upon subsoil conditions, foundation type, and method of construction, structural issues can become important in disposition situations.

Real Estate Brokers

The disposition of corporate property usually requires the services of a qualified broker. A good broker should understand corporate disposition, especially the corporate approval process. Many corporations are averse to using a broker because they do not want to pay commissions. This is false reasoning, however, because the broker can devote considerable energy and time to marketing unwanted property. Part of the process usually involves exposure of the property to multiple markets. The broker can accomplish this much more effectively and efficiently than the corporate real estate manager.

There are several essential elements in a good brokerage relationship:

1. *Listing agreement.* Without a listing agreement, a broker does not have adequate incentive to perform for a client. The agreement should be an exclusive agency contract. It should provide the broker with sufficient time to market the property effectively. The agreement should provide for compensation based on actual results.

2. *Documentation.* In addition to having a specific written summation of work performed, the broker should document inquiries about each property. Literature should be developed for marketing each property. The broker may screen prospects for the corporation. This process should also be documented for the real estate disposition manager.

Brokers do have a role in the disposition process. The corporate manager should use brokers to maximize the market exposure which the property will receive.

Legal Advice

The importance of retaining the best legal counsel available in a disposition matter cannot be overemphasized. Legal fees are a minor part of the cost of disposition, and worth it. Some corporations have their own staff counsel. In complex disposition situations, corporate counsel should be supplemented by outside counsel, especially if the property is in a distant city. Outside counsel can be invaluable in assisting negotiations; providing interpretation of local building, zoning, and fire codes; assisting in acquiring permits; and expediting the closing of a transaction. They serve as an adjunct to the corporate attorney, who may be working on several matters at once, without the time to focus on a single disposition issue. If many properties are involved, outside counsel is vital because the work load is normally too much for a typical corporate legal staff.

Dispositions are at least as legally complex as acquisitions. Of particular significance are the following:

1. *Sales Contracts.*   The sale of corporate assets normally requires approval of executive committees and often boards of directors. The contracts, therefore, require sufficient conditional language to protect the selling corporation in the event these approvals are not forthcoming. Additionally, the sale of corporate real estate requires adequate timetables for due diligence, approval of mortgages for the sale or assumption of financing, approval of signatories of reciprocal operating and easement agreements, complex calculations of operating expenses, and provisions for default on the part of buyer and seller, which are normally tied to complex formulas.

2. *Leaseholds.*   Leases may be assigned or sublet. There are legal conditions precedent to these actions that may require particular legal skills. For example, although a lease may contain an assignment clause, the ability to assign may be hampered by an operating covenant. These covenants are particularly troublesome if they are "named" covenants, where the lessee has agreed to operate a facility under a trade name for a period of years. They are further complicated by the fact that a mortgage may require that these covenants be kept in place. Leasehold provisions in a sublease situation are also important. In a sublease the parties will negotiate priorities that protect the sublessor corporation from problems which may arise in the subtenant's company. The profits of the sublease also need to be protected from claims by the lessor on the primary lease. Subleases may also be written as subsidies, where the subtenant actually pays less than the contract rent paid by the sublessor. In a retail sublease situation, the lessee may be forced to pay a rent that is equal to the base rent plus some average of percentage rent which had been previously paid. The attorney has to be prepared for this trap and the real estate manager has to negotiate this into the subrent.

In planning for a disposition, the legal counsel and the real estate manager need to operate as a team to achieve the desired results.

Concluding the Disposition

Once a disposition plan has been adopted, many pressures come to bear on completion of the plan.

Controlling the Process

All dispositions of major corporate assets involve a role for the corporate public relations department. The timing of the closing of a facility is critical for preserving the corporate reputation. Real estate and other departments must work together so that public and employee concerns are addressed.

To complete a deal properly, the corporate real estate manager should have a detailed schedule of all materials required for the closing and a timetable for the coordinated delivery of these materials. Wiring instructions for banks should be clear and exact. Title companies should be aware of their role, and lines of communication to both sides in the closing need to be kept open. Corporate officers who must execute the various closing documents should keep their schedules clear and be flexible enough to allow for last-minute modifications of documents.

Corporate departments other than real estate should be ready to fulfill their assigned responsibilities. Engineering groups, for example, should be prepared to transfer utilities on the correct day, and any items of restoration or new construction that were agreed to should have been completed. Trade fixtures or other inventory should have been removed from the facility. Railroad or trucking agreements should have been transferred or canceled, as well as contracts for HVAC, vertical transportation, security, and fire protection.

Maximizing Results

Disposition is the end of a process that will have taken several months to several years. It is a process that requires perseverance and patience. The pressures placed upon a corporate real estate disposition manager to divest often hamper the process. Buyers understand this and use this knowledge to their best advantage. Corporate management must realize that surplus real estate can be a valuable asset. It can be made to perform well, given time and the correct market environment. Personnel handling asset disposition should be given the necessary support from the top to maximize results.

Index